SHOWBUSINESS

SHOWBUSINESS

Diary of a Rock'n'Roll Nobody

Mark Radcliffe

SCEPTRE

Grateful acknowledgement is made for permission to reprint excerpts
from the following copyrighted works:
'Ghost Town' by Jerry Dammers © 1981
Plangent Visions Music Limited

'Get It On' by Marc Bolan © 1971 Westminster Music Ltd of Suite 2.07,
Plaza 535 Kings Rd, London SW10 0SZ. International copyright secured.
All rights reserved. Used by permission.

First published in 1998 by Hodder and Stoughton
A division of Hodder Headline PLC
A Sceptre book

10 9 8 7 6 5 4 3 2 1

British Library C.I.P.
A CIP catalogue record for this title is available
from the British Library

ISBN 0 340 71566 9

Typeset by Palimpsest Book Production Limited,
Polmont, Stirlingshire

Printed and bound in Great Britain by
Clays Ltd, St Ives plc

Hodder and Stoughton
A division of Hodder Headline PLC
338 Euston Road
London NW1 3BH

For B and H and the ghost of Jimmy L

Acknowledgements

Thanks to my mum and dad who bought me the drums and put up with the noise for years, as did Jaine and Joe. Thanks to Matthew and Andy for the day job and Jeanne and Ian at East West for helping to take the joke too far. Thanks to Angela at Hodder who believed a disc jockey could construct a sentence. Thanks to everyone in the bands, especially Phil and Marc. Finally thanks to Bella for love, support and, not least, typing.

1

The Berlin Airlift

It's an addiction. Simple as that. For most of my adolescent and adult life I've had to accept its hold over me. There have been times when I've tried to fight it, but resistance is futile. It's an addiction and that's all there is to it.

Most kids have at least a vague idea of what they want to do when they grow up. My idea was anything but vague: I wanted to be in a band. I've been in so many bands for so much of my life that it's hard to say how it all began. I can remember as a little kid being very keen on a television programme called *The White Heather Club*, which was a weekly showcase of Scottish music. So great was my enthusiasm for imitating the jigs and reels that my mum ran me up a kilt out of an old travelling rug. Donning it religiously five minutes before Robin Hall and Jimmy McGregor and the rest of the *White Heather* regulars came on became a familiar ritual, and I've come to look on this as an early expression of the desire to become a musical performer. At least, it doesn't appear to have been an early expression of the desire to become Scottish.

It was at my grandma and grandad's house in Farnworth

that I became a drummer. Every Sunday afternoon, after the remains of the cold brisket, onions in vinegar and sherry trifle had been put back in the pantry, my grandad would turn on the radiogramme to make sure the valves were warmed up in time for *Pick of the Pops* presented by Alan Freeman. Meanwhile, I would run round the house snatching various appliances and small pieces of furniture with which to construct a makeshift drum-kit: a suedette pouffe for a bass drum, a pan lid for a cymbal, a washing-up bowl in lieu of a snare. Suitably prepared, I would then spend a blissful hour clattering the aged household effects with splintering knitting needles while the rest of the family drew closer to the telly in order to hear *Songs of Praise* above the smash-and-grab swoop on an ironmonger's that was taking place in the front parlour. Eventually my mum and dad bought me a couple of real drums, probably on the assumption that it was a cheaper option than constantly replacing grandma's ovenware, and once I had the drums I had to have the band. And that's how it all started. I've been in dodgy bands with dodgy names ever since, and the first of these was the Berlin Airlift.

I was fourteen at the time and in daily attendance at the imposing sandstone establishment known as Bolton School, an admirably christened institution, being, as it was, a school in Bolton. Under the occasionally watchful eye of Mr Derbyshire we were tracing the course of the Second World War, and the name of the band was taken from the index of a history textbook, having been selected from a shortlist that also included Polish Corridor, Warsaw Pact, Scapa Flow and the Warmington-on-Sea Home Guard. The latter was suggested as a joke at the time, but with the benefit of hindsight and the eventual realisation that we were a bunch of rank amateurs with no chance of achieving anything, it now looks by far the most appropriate. Another short-lived contender was Derbyshire Is a Git. Despite being a bewitching name for a beat combo, however, it didn't really count, because it hadn't actually been printed in the index but scrawled there by Carl Walters, and as Mr Derbyshire was not only our housemaster but also the bloke who booked the bands for the school disco, we quickly dismissed that option, tempting though it was. Take it from me, you'll never get anywhere in showbusiness if you insult the promoter. Your chances of playing Wembley will be severely dented if you insist on calling yourselves Short-Arse 'Arvey Goldsmith and the Little Fat Bearded Bastards.

The members of the Berlin Airlift are now, of course, the stuff of rock legend and Pete Frame Family Tree. For those unfamiliar with the full epic saga, and I can't think there are many, I can only point you in the direction of Albert Goldman's incisive critique, *From Bolton School to the Budokhan – Berlin Airlift: The Wonder Years*. The list of former Airlifters who went on to become musicians of international repute is too long and fictitious to print here, but if I were to mention names like Jeff 'Carry' Carrington, Mark 'Stocky' Sayers and Michael 'Doris' Lipsey you'll understand the calibre of artist we're dealing with.

Undoubtedly, though, the true Airlift aficionado will always hark back to the original line-up, the seminal four-piece whose blend of glam and metal sent reverberations not only through my sister's bedroom but out on to Carlton Road if she had the window open. So who were these four kick-botty horsemen of the rock'n'roll apocalypse, meticulously honing an act that would one day take them all the way to Bolton Lad's Club at the bottom of Chorley New Road? Well, for starters, there was me on drums and lead vocals.

Many people find the concept of singing drummers an odd one, but you have to remember that archangel Peter Gabriel was still the front man with Genesis at this time. This kept the Artful Codger Phil 'Buster' Collins in his rightful place behind the kit, so no one really knew how deeply unpleasant the phenomenon of the vocalising tub-thumper would prove to be. It's also been suggested that it's not exactly a riveting visual feast for the audience if the lead singer is hidden behind what looks like the contents of a small hardware emporium. I'm not convinced that this is a bad thing – have you seen Simple Minds? Personally I think it's infinitely preferable to have a vocalist who's pretty much invisible rather than some podgy ponce in a girlie blouse prancing up and down the stage shouting 'Woooah . . . do you feel all right . . . let me see some hands.'

So there was me on drums and vocals, and on a good day I would assess my musical ability, out of a possible ten, as two.

Then there was Jerry Lumley on guitar. Jerry was a rocker in the Leslie West, Screaming Trees, Tad and Meatloaf mould. He was fat. In a school riddled with zit-infested budding pop stars, Jerry Lumley looked the least likely ever to walk on stage to be greeted by a thousand adolescent screams and a barrage of moist pubescent underwear. He had one major advantage over the rest of us, though: he could actually play. He could play T Rex tunes and Bowie tunes and Beatles tunes; he could even play the 'Moonlight' Sonata on the piano, although sadly it never figured in our blistering live set. Had we gone in more of a progressive rock direction, we would no doubt have had a pseudo-classical interlude in the middle of our epic anthem to teen angst, 'I can't go to Yates's 'cos I've not been paid for my paper round'. At a given point, probably a smoke bomb, the blimp-like Lumley would put down his guitar, stride majestically to the piano, toss his Lurex cape back and hammer out a few bars of 'Moonlight' gubbins before launching into his own baroque composition, 'Night Dance of the Fire Pixies'. Alas, he never got the chance. And the title had probably been used by Rush anyway.

So there was me on drums and vocals, musical ability out of ten, on a good day: two; Jerry Lumley on guitar, musical ability: five or even six; and there was another guitarist by the name of Guy Farringdon. At this stage in our lives you have to remember that the word 'guitarist' meant someone who owned a guitar and not necessarily someone who could play it. With a wicked bit of schoolboy irony we dubbed him Eric, after Eric Clapton, so it's now doubly ironic that as head of his family food empire Guy Farringdon appeared above Eric Clapton in the *Sunday Times* league table of the UK's two hundred richest men.

As you can imagine, given his background, Guy (or Eric) wasn't short of a bob or two, but he was in the band for two reasons. First, he had a Watkins Rapier. Now, if you're thinking that this is a typical bit of rich-kid lunacy, owning a car before legally being able to drive, then you're getting confused with the Sunbeam Rapier. The Watkins Rapier 44 was, and I'll pause here for a gasp of incredulity . . . an electric guitar – something we'd only ever seen on television or by pressing our noses against shop windows, and we saw a lot more of them when we started pressing our noses against music-shop windows and moved on from the butcher's. They've stopped making Watkins guitars now, so they've become highly sought-after collectors' items, which means that they still sound bloody awful but the price has gone up a lot.

It wouldn't be fair to say that Guy (or Eric) couldn't play the guitar at all – he could strum chords with no less ineptitude than most of us – but he was nowhere near as good as Jerry Lumley. This presented no initial problem as it was always accepted that Jez would be the free-flowing lead axe hero of the organisation with Guy clanking in on rhythm when he was 80 to 90 per cent sure he'd got his fingers in the right places. However, there was a flaw in this arrangement that only became apparent during rehearsals for our glamorous début booking. The dextrous Lumley had only an acoustic guitar, an Eko Ranger 6 for all you trainspotters out there, while the ham-fisted Farringdon had not only the coveted Watkins but also a tinnitus-inducing Vox AC30 amplifier. Flash git. The average Airlift number consequently consisted of Jerry and I starting more or less together and making a reasonable job of the first line before being completely drowned out as our esteemed rhythm ace decided to risk a howitzer chord. The chorus of Slade's 'Cum On Feel the Noize', for instance, would take the form:

So cum on feel the . . . *KERRAAANGG-G-G*

Girls grab the *KERCHUUUNGG-G-G.*

Soon realising that this was going to get pretty tiresome for those unfortunate enough to have been press-ganged into the audience, Jerry tentatively suggested an exchange of instruments, just for the forthcoming appearance naturally.

Guy (Eric) was less than tentative in telling Jez to stuff his Eko Ranger up his arse. Which, for a lad of Jez's build, was by no means an impossibility.

The second reason that Guy Farringdon (Eric Clapton) was enlisted was to bring some much-needed sex appeal to the ranks. These days he looks every inch the dapper captain of industry, but back then he had tousled white beach-bum locks, in contrast to Jerry Lumley, who had a bum the size of a beach. He also had a luscious peaches-and-cream complexion, in contrast to me, who had a fruit-salad complexion necessitating Clearasil on draught. This made him something of a heart-throb to our school's lower-sixth-form pupils. It was even rumoured that girls fancied him as well. In fact, he and I later risked the whole existence of the band as we competed for the attentions of Pippa Johnson. Initially the flaxen-haired strum-meister won out, only for her to realise that money, good looks and charm aren't everything, and you're often better off with a weedy, penniless drummer with a pudding-basin fringe concealing a forehead full of acne. In the end she moved down south and became with child to a bloke who worked for Siemens.

To recap, then, I was on drums and vocals, musical ability: two; there was Jerry Lumley on increasingly inaudible lead guitar, musical ability: five or even six; there was Guy Farringdon on ear-drum-threatening rhythm guitar and pout, musical ability: one; and there was Davey Bright. Davey Bright could fix things with a soldering iron and so seemed eminently well qualified to be the roadie. Why, then, we gave him the bass player's job I'll never know. The fact that he couldn't play bass at all wasn't immediately apparent as he didn't own one. To be fair to him, I don't recall him ever claiming he could play. In retrospect I think we may have forced him into it, approaching, as we were, a prestigious concert recital under the misapprehension that the classic four-piece line-up is: vocals, drums, guitar, bass. It isn't. When starting a band you should remember that the classic four-piece line-up is: vocals, drums, guitar, van driver. You can be the finest undiscovered band in the universe, but you're liable to stay that way for a very long time if you can't get your gear to the gig.

Practically talentless and emphatically vanless, the full line-up was in place: me on drums and vocals, musical ability: two; Jerry Lumley on adept but inaudible guitar, musical ability: five or even six; Guy Farringdon on inept and noisy guitar, musical ability: one; and Davey Bright on soldering iron and a bass that was still in the shop, musical ability: zero. How could we fail?

'Good evening, Lostock Tennis Club – are you ready to rock?'

The pavilion of Lostock Tennis Club was a shed on stilts where posh kids and their parents drank Pimm's after another rubber or whatever they call it. As the world's dullest and most pointless game apart from golf, the ins and outs of tennis need not detain us here. It's the rock heritage of the Lostock Clubhouse that's important. We were booked to play by some posh kid's dad who was the social secretary. Looking back on it, this could be viewed as an act of great philanthropy, giving four struggling young lads a chance to show what they could do, even if it wasn't much. In reality I think it's more likely that he was pissed when Guy asked him.

Like the Beatles at the Cavern, the Sex Pistols at the 100 Club or Roger Whitaker at the Tameside Theatre, Ashton-under-Lyne, if everyone who now claims to have been at Lostock Tennis Club that night actually had been there we'd have filled the Albert Hall. Not the Royal Albert Hall down south, the Albert Hall in Bolton, where we would later witness such greats as Trapeze, Judas Priest and the Dawn Dawson Academy of Song and Dance's 'Young Stars of Tomorrow'.

We arrived at the club around lunch-time. At least, three of us did. Jerry and I took the drums and the Eko Ranger with us on the bus, while Davey somehow managed to get his newly purchased bass, his amplifier and his soldering kit there on his bike. The maestro Eric had warned us he couldn't make it till around two-thirty. I forget what he was doing, but I suspect it was one of those peculiar pastimes that only the children of the wealthy seem to indulge in and which remain utterly mystifying to the rest of us. Things like elocution and deportment lessons and rugby sevens.

He duly arrived on the dot of an hour and a half later than he'd promised, bounding into the room, Watkins in hand, leaving his arthritic mother to haul the AC30 from the boot of the Jaguar and up the rickety wooden staircase that was in itself a part of rock'n'roll history. It has been widely rumoured that the working title for Led Zeppelin's 'Stairway to Heaven' was in fact 'Stairway to Lostock Tennis Club', but I've been unable to verify this with Jimmy Page or Robert Plant at time of going to press. How these people get where they are without returning phone calls is beyond me.

The first thing that would have struck Guy on his belated arrival in the clubhouse that day was the size of my newly

9

embellished drum-kit. Well, that's not strictly true. The first thing to strike him would have been Jerry Lumley's fist, had not the bar steward intervened with a placatory 'Now, now, lads' and the promise of free halves of Watney's dark mild when the pumps were turned on. Nevertheless, my battery of percussion was impressive, to say the least – and preposterous, to say the most. For the last few years my mum and dad had been buying me a drum every Christmas and birthday, so I had pretty much a full kit by the time the gig arrived. Ever restless, though, I decided the set-up looked a little on the tentative side, so I went up to Barry Halpern's place to borrow a few extra tom-toms.

Barry Halpern was a school friend of mine who had a big penis. This is not some frank confession of an adolescent homosexual liaison, it was just that everyone knew he had a big penis because he always had it out in class. And I think if I'd had one of comparable size I'd have been as keen to show it off as he was. On one memorable occasion during physics, Mr McCarroll spotted the affable Halpern fiddling with something under the desk. Not knowing what sort of monster was lurking down there, the exasperated and long-suffering McCarroll ejaculated, 'Halpern, whatever you're messing with, bring it out here to me.' That Barry Halpern cheerfully obliged cemented his place in our hearts for ever, and the hours spent moulding and toying with his hot and malleable lump proved, in later life, to be time well spent, as he became a blacksmith.

In truth he was a bit of a rough diamond. That's to say he was thoroughly disreputable but quite likeable on the days he wasn't psychotically unhinged. He wasn't a drummer, but I knew he had some drums; just as he wasn't a guitarist, trombonist, gardener, chef or stunt motorcyclist, but he had a guitar, trombone, a Flymo, a Moulinex Multichef and a BSA Bantam 500. I never knew for sure that the drums were stolen, but I do remember thinking it odd that they were stored under a tarpaulin in the bushes at the back of his house.

So, thanks to my covert relationship with the well-hung mastermind of Bolton's schoolboy underworld, I had thirteen drums arranged around me. They were matched only in that they all sounded dreadful, but it didn't matter. I had the biggest drum-kit out of anybody at our school, and for the next gig I planned to get some cymbals.

If Jerry Lumley had taken the time to cultivate a friendship with Barry Halpern he wouldn't have suffered the indignities that he suffered that night. If he'd just taken the trouble to buy him the odd bottle of cider and admire his penis with the rest of us, then Barry would have found him an electric guitar, no bother. As it was, he had his Eko Ranger 6 jumbo acoustic, on to which had been fitted a pathetic-looking pick-up with two jumbo knobs marked 'tone' and 'volume'. When he strapped this contraption on to his jumbo belly he near as dammit filled the dance floor on his own. As if this wasn't enough, he had another cross to bear. He had no amplifier. This meant he had to plug his guitar directly into the PA system. The term PA system probably conjures up the same image for most of us: improbably high piles of industrial container-sized cabinets that stand like prehistoric monoliths at the side of the stage. At Lostock Tennis Club the PA system consisted of two speakers that could feasibly have been removed from telephone answering machines, hurriedly installed in a pair of wooden cigar boxes and nailed to the wall. More usually this equipment would have been used by the bingo caller or perhaps, because it was a middle-class venue, by the master of ceremonies at the mah-jong evening. Whichever, it was tinny and crackly and feeble and not what Jerry Lumley had in mind to launch his glittering rock career.

Davey Bright, on the other hand, stood proudly in front of a rack of speaker cabinets that put even Guy Farringdon's AC30 to shame. All afternoon, he'd gone to and from his house ferrying, in ever-increasing sizes, a succession of boxes with wires trailing from them. This primitive but superhuman feat of patient construction made you wonder if he hadn't had a previous incarnation as a site foreman in the Valley of the Kings. There was still nothing to suggest he'd had a previous incarnation as a bass player, but he was a trooper, I'll say that for him. The reason this elaborate assembly had to be completed in stages was two-fold. For a start there's only so many cabinets you can carry on a drop-handlebar racer at one time, and secondly he had to wait for his parents to go out before dismantling his dad's hi-fi and making off with the Wharfedale Super Lintons.

Eventually his wall of bass bins included his dad's sizeable Wharfedales, his own stereo speakers boasting the legend 'Saisho' and two hessian-covered boxes of indeterminate origin from which no audible sound ever emanated despite, or possibly because of, the hours he spent tinkering inside them with a soldering iron. All in all, it was a pretty impressive 'stack', especially for someone who was going to spend the entire set turned off because he couldn't play yet. This left him free to do what he did really well – shake his hair about.

No self-respecting band embroiled in the throbbing glam-metal scene of the early to mid-seventies would have dared to take the stage without at least one lank-haired tosspot apparently in the advanced stages of Parkinson's disease, and ours was Davey Bright. From the opening chords of the first number until the final shout of 'You've been a great audience, we'll see you again real soon, we're Berlin Airlift, and Colin, your mum's waiting in the Chevette outside, goodnight!' the rubber-necked Bright would toss his ginger mane continuously. Personally I thought he could have stopped during the interminable inter-song tuning breaks, but once he started he was in a world of his own. He would have come desperately close to looking cool – well, as cool as a fifteen-year-old crater-faced ginger bollocks in bicycle clips can look – were it not for two things. For a start, everyone knows that the size of a guitarist's speaker stack is a penis substitute, so you could only assume he had a button mushroom in his pants. Perhaps Jerry Lumley was banking on the collective assumption that, as he had no amplifier at all, he was in a position to cross swords with Barry Halpern. And on top of Bright's wall of speakers, clearly visible to the audience, was a large illustrated book titled *How to Play the Bass Guitar*. This was doubly stupid, because not only did it blow any semblance of respect he might have had, but for that night's proceedings he didn't need to know how to play the bass guitar. All he needed to know could be found in two other books in the same series, namely, *How to Hold the Bass Guitar* and *How to Shake the Greasy Barnet*. Still, as the old muso proverb goes, 'You can lead a horse to water, but you can't stop the bass player making a dick of himself.'

So the stage was set for, if you will, lift-off. Thirteen

battered drums took centre stage flanked on one side by a Vox AC30 and on the other by what looked like the haul from a ram raid on Tandy's. All we could do was wait.

Each of us had our own pre-gig ritual. I would drink as many free halves of Watney's dark mild as I possibly could in the hope of avoiding stage fright. All I ultimately avoided were the girls who came to chat casually to the band after the gig, as I was otherwise engaged vomiting casually into a bucket. Guy, on the other hand, would spend his time talking amiably, with the confidence only a large trust fund can bring, to a succession of drop-dead-gorgeous hard-bodied honeys in tennis skirts. Well, each to their own; he might have cleaned up with the totty, but I drank his ale while he was at it. That showed him. Davey Bright was far too busy soldering things to be interested in girls or beer, and Jerry Lumley remained aloof and enigmatic, by which I mean he sat on his own looking grumpy between trips to the lavatory to shit through the eye of a needle. Soon enough we were summoned to take our positions, and on to the stage shuffled the drummer who'd drunk too much, the bass player who'd soldered his fingers together, the guitarist with the raging hard-on and the guitarist with the debilitating diarrhoea. 'Hi, chicks – we're the Berlin Airlift.'

The posh kid's pissed posh dad who'd booked us took it upon himself to give us a big showbiz introduction. Lumbering on to the stage in his Pringle sweater and gardening corduroys, with his hair combed over from some indeterminate point behind his left ear, and pausing only to liberally slop Vermouth over the main power supply, he grabbed the only microphone and said, 'Now, then, boys and girls, there'll be bowls of piping hot-pot all round later on, but first some up-tempo beat music from four young men from Bolton School – Berlin Chairlift!'

As a call to arms it was hardly 'Kick out the jams, motherfuckers', but we were on. Almost. Because there was only one microphone, there was an agonising wait while this pillock in pastel knitwear shuffled round the stage trying to position it for the singer behind the wall of drums. It may have been only a short pause, but in it there was enough time for Davey Bright to finally separate his fingers with a posi-drive screwdriver, for Guy Farringdon to thrust his crotch out and wink knowingly at someone by the bar (bastard, I bet it's Pippa Johnson), for me to belch voluminously and for Jerry Lumley to fart catastrophically into the arse of his ill-fitting brushed-denim flares. We'd chosen to start with the T. Rex gem 'Get It On' because not only was it a sure-fire crowd pleaser, being a big hit-parade smash of the day, but it also kept the Farringdon big guns on hold until at least some of the audience had recognised the song we were mangling. Gig one, song one; one, two, three . . .

> Well, you're dirty and sweet, clad in black, don't look
>   back, and I love you . . .
> You're dirty and sweet, oh yeah . . .
> Well, you're slim and you're weak, got the teeth of a
>   hydra upon you . . .
> You're dirty sweet and you're my girl . . .
> Get it KERPLLAANGGG . . .
> Bang a KERRFLLUUUNGG . . .
> Get it KERROOINGGGG.

15

The fact that the cocksure Farringdon looked so blissfully unaware of the damage his lunatic shards of noise were inflicting on the sensitive ears of the assembled minors only added to the general air of bemusement. The benign coffin dodger who'd come along to serve the hot-pot had evidently been tapping a sensible walking shoe quite happily until gunner Eric let her have it with both barrels, at which point she coughed her false teeth straight into the red cabbage.

'Get Back' came next, followed by the Move's 'California Man' and Mott the Hoople's 'Honaloochie Boogie', by which time the audience had begun to see a pattern emerging and knew to brace themselves during the choruses. Jerry Lumley was bracing himself as well, although from where I was sitting it looked a little late for that.

So much for the aural feast that was the Berlin Airlift, but what of the visuals? Davey Bright's frenzied fringe-flinging was proving immensely popular stage left as with each forceful flop he dipped a foppish frond into a pint of best bitter on a stage-front table. (The pint remained, unsurprisingly, unclaimed until later, when I, equally unsurprisingly, downed it in one before, least surprisingly of all, spewing it up at the base of the umpire's chair while Guy Farringdon was snogging for England.) The spectacle stage right basically consisted of Guy attempting to look effortlessly cool, despite the front row's detection of a deeply unpleasant aroma, which they had no way of knowing originated in Jerry Lumley's trousers.

The other weapon we had in our eye-catching arsenal was the celebrated Airlift light show. This consisted of a string of coloured bulbs, wired up by Davey Bright and operated by a contact cunningly fashioned from two strips of Meccano. The idea was to connect this elaborate device to the bass drum pedal so the lights would flash in time to what I hesitate to call the music. There was absolutely nothing wrong with this in principle apart from the fact that our fifth number, an ill-advised stab at Black Sabbath's 'Solitude', featured me on bass and vocals and therefore no drums at all. If K–Tel ever put together a compilation album called *Now That's What I Call Music to Burn Coffins By, Volume One* or *The Most Thoroughly Depressing Album in the World . . . Ever*, then side one, track one will be Black Sabbath's 'Solitude'. Why we decided to subject people to this suicidal dirge is a mystery to me now, although it does contain only two chords, which probably made us feel reasonably confident about getting through it. Even we realised, though, that to subject people to this suicidal dirge in total darkness was not what you might call a guaranteed winner. There was even, given the satanic nature of the Sabbath *oeuvre*, the risk of an outbreak of junior devil worship. The last thing we wanted was to turn the lights back on to find that a young virgin, of which there were plenty to hand, had been ritually sacrificed on the buffet table by a demonically possessed Barry Halpern.

If we'd had a way of getting in touch with Roger Waters or Dave Gilmour out of Pink Floyd, we could have asked for some advice on what to do with the special effects to keep the audience awake during the dull bits. Unfortunately their numbers weren't in the Bolton phone book, which, with the benefit of hindsight, I realise they wouldn't be. Members of a big band like that were bound to be ex-directory. Thankfully, Guy Farringdon, the clever one, showed the ingenuity and leadership that's made him the wealthy entrepreneur he is today: 'For Christ's sake, just get someone else to work the lights, then,' he shrieked with a hint of the frustration that is inevitable when it finally dawns on you that you're involved with people you wouldn't trust to sit the right way round on the toilet.

Accordingly my corpulent cousin Bernie Ryman sat next to the drum-kit operating the Lostock Illuminations throughout the gig. To those of us in the know, this was the perfect solution, but his presence in the line-up only added to the audience's growing sense of bewilderment. Because Bernie's entire responsibilities entailed pressing a small pedal, as far as the paying public were concerned there was a blond-bobbed lard-arse in a Suzi Quatro T-shirt sitting centre stage tapping his foot. This, of course, was long before Andrew Ridgely and Bez had been invented, so the concept of having a member of the band who doesn't do anything was still uncharted territory. As if this wasn't bad enough for the rotund Ryman, our technical wizard Davey Bright had unwittingly wired the apparatus so that each contact of the pedal discharged a small blast of electric current through the operator's blubbery leg. No wonder he looked miserable, although not as miserable as Jerry Lumley, who'd been uninvolved in the great lighting debate as he had other things on his mind. And on the back of his underpants. In later life Davey Bright became the safety officer for a factory in Nottingham. For the sake of the work-force, I hope his knowledge of circuitry improved.

Still, we had sound, we had light and the mid-set wrist-slitting interlude was over. Playing our remaining four songs at ever-increasing tempo in a desperate rush for the bar (me), the lavatory (Jerry Lumley), the fuse box (Davey Bright), Pippa Johnson's pants (Guy Farringdon) and the Bolton Royal Infirmary casualty department (Bernie 'Rubberlegs'

Ryman), we hurtled through Status Quo's 'Big Fat Mama' and David Bowie's 'Gene Jeanie', before hurriedly climaxing with 'Johnny B. Goode' and 'Summertime Blues'. As a grand finale the Eddie Cochran standard was a particularly bad move. Most of our songs were only sporadically subjected to Eric's artillery bombardment; in 'Summertime Blues' he opened fire indiscriminately, pausing only for the celebrated chorus breaks. The by-now-zombified audience's lasting memory of the Berlin Airlift was thus

'KERRAAAAAANNG . . . KERRRTHRONNNG . . .
KERRDDDUUUNG . . . KERRRBLLINNGG . . .

Ain't no cure for the summertime blues . . .

KRREENNGGG . . . KRRROINNGGG . . .
KKRRUUNGGG . . . KERRRPLAAAANNNG . . .

followed by me shouting 'Thank you, Lostock, you've been a wonderful audience – Colin, your mum's waiting in the Chevette outside – we're the Berlin Airlift . . . goodnight', followed by Bernie Ryman shouting 'Jesus Christ, my bloody leg's on fire.'

We didn't get an encore. I think this was because it was past the curfew for live music, what with it being nine forty-five and everything.

Six months on from this auspicious début Guy left Bolton to go to a posh school down south. After much soul searching we decided we couldn't carry on without him, principally because he was taking his AC30 with him, although we later betrayed him by re-forming with some blokes who had part shares in a Selmer valve amp. During those intervening months we would rehearse sporadically, improve marginally and perform occasionally at such celebrated rock venues as Bolton Lads' Club, Eagley Tennis Club and, most legendary of all, the Parochial Hall on Markland Hill, which sadly for the legions of would-be sightseers has long since been sacrilegiously demolished.

Davey Bright eventually found the confidence to turn his bass guitar on, Jerry Lumley never owned an amplifier and Bernie Ryman never came to see us again. Some of our other gigs drew less embarrassingly small crowds, some of our gigs were less plagued with technical hitches and teeth-jarring bum notes, but we never felt our nerve ends, or in Jerry's case sphincter muscles, tingle again like they did that first night.

2

Billy Moon

Shortly after the demise of the Berlin Airlift (Mark I) we began to go and watch proper gigs, and the first two were Judas Priest and David Bowie. Both would prove to have a powerful effect on our plans for future world domination, although for profoundly different reasons.

For the uninitiated, and think yourselves lucky, Judas Priest are a leather-clad, ham-fisted, club-footed heavy-metal band of no fixed ability from the West Midlands. Moderately successful in the Walsall area, they inexplicably became a platinum-selling act in America in the late seventies and early eighties, particularly in those states whose only function appears to be keeping interesting states further apart on the map. You'd have thought life in a one-horse-trough town in the backwoods of Iowa was bad enough without listening to Judas Priest as well.

The Priest, as we people who've never met them in our lives insist on calling them, have come to be remembered principally for a couple of things. Their lead singer was called Rob Halford. With a perfectly healthy interest in Satan, leather and the odd sad wing of destiny, Rob Halford would be your average everyday gravel-throated rock vocalist but for the fact that he's bald. The man is a roll-on deodorant in leathers. Personally I've always felt sorry for the follicularly challenged in heavy metal because headbanging without luxuriant tresses is one of the funniest things you'll see outside of a Jimmy Nail concert. Everyone has at some point seen a third-rate metal band rocking out, biker boots propped up on the monitors, with the lead singer tossing his leonine mane, the two guitarists trading licks in a blur of poodle perms, Louis XIV flailing away behind the drum-kit and the rapidly thinning bass player's comb-over dangling sweat-soaked at the side of his head like a drizzle-drenched windsock at some God-forsaken disused aerodrome off the A1. If you want proof, get some early videos of Saxon, although you'll spare yourself a lot of unpleasantness if you just take my word for it. Obviously conscious of his lack of cool, the Uncle Fester-like Rob Halford at one time decided to give himself a bit of stage presence by cruising on to the concert platform astride his beloved Harley Davidson. This went well until the night he confused the brake for the throttle and, roaring majestically from the wings stage right, failed to stop majestically stage centre, instead roaring less than majestically straight off stage left, where a collision with a disgruntled monitor engineer called Spike awaited. Top-flight comedy.

Apart from the bald Barry Sheen of the Brummie band scene there's not much else of interest to say about Judas Priest, and they would undoubtedly be but a footnote in the annals of rock were it not for one key event. In 1985 in deepest Nevada two adolescents attempted a shotgun suicide pact, which one of them survived, after the repeated playing of a Judas Priest album. Well, eager to escape the sonic torture, most of us would have simply taken a cigarette lighter and refashioned the vinyl artefact as an ornamental plant pot, but you can imagine how they felt. The whole affair might have ended there, were it not for a bizarre court case in which the boys' parents attempted to sue the band for damages on account of the demonic messages placed subliminally within their songs. The understandably distraught families insisted that Rob Halford had peppered the Priest preposteropus with backwards slogans from the Prince of Darkness encouraging the impressionable young-sters to blow their brains out. This always seemed unlikely to me. For starters, would a band who'd achieved success beyond their wildest dreams get involved in a scheme to systematically eradicate their fan base? I think not, and, in any case, if Satan wanted to get a message to the youth of the world it seems odd that he would put it backwards at low volume in a Judas Priest album track. In terms of getting your manifesto across, you're leaving an awful lot to chance there, as I'm sure the Mephistophelean campaign management team told him. If you'd been the satanic spin doctor, wouldn't you have told him to hang fire and damnation and do a future deal with the Spice Girls? Thankfully, common sense prevailed and the Priest were cleared of any dark dealings or wrongdoings, but not before the trial descended into pure farce. At one point the judge asked the grieving mums and dads if they'd noticed any abnormal behaviour in their hirsute offspring before their tragic deaths. Well, of course they had, the idiots had been locked in the bedroom listening to Judas Priest. If that's not abnormal, I don't know what is.

Thankfully, that night in Bolton Albert Hall Judas Priest

inspired in us a different kind of hysteria. That of uncontrollable laughter. From their turgid songs and self-indulgent solos to their clod-hopping platform boots and charmless vocalist caterwauling 'Whisky Woman Way-ay-ay', they provided an evening of unrelenting, if unintentional, comedy. We were young and impressionable and we'd never seen a real band before, but even we thought they were rubbish. We came out of that gig wiping the tears from our eyes and totally convinced about one thing. We didn't know what our new band was going to be like, but it was definitely going to be nothing like Judas Priest.

Several weeks later came a gig that would leave us slack-jawed in awe and admiration. David Bowie, and in particular the *Ziggy Stardust* album, had for some months captured our imaginations like no previous record. Night after night we pored over the sleeve looking for hitherto undiscovered twists in the lyrics as the eponymous rock'n'roll hero descended into tragedy and suicide. Perhaps he'd been locked in his bedroom listening to Judas Priest. The combination of Bowie's stories and singing, interspersed with the razor slashes of the late Mick Ronson's guitar, provided a cocktail that still seems pretty potent to me, but there was more to it than that.

There was the sexual ambivalence for a start: was Bowie straight? Was he gay? Was he bisexual? Was he in fact a woman? This last question was to all intents and purposes answered when we saw a picture of him on-stage in what looked like a Japanese-print bathing costume with, unless he'd taken to carrying slices of bacon about in his pants, one dangling testicle easing itself out of the skimpy and overtight gusset. You have to remember that none of us had travelled much. If we had been familiar with the fleshpots of Bangkok we'd have known that there were all kinds of hybrids that could further complicate matters and that the possession of a pair of bollocks was by no means a guarantee that their owner was 100 per cent male. However, we were pretty confident that Bowie was a bloke, but the next question to be addressed was whether or not he was a bloke from another world? His songs were sprinkled with references to space and starmen, and what's more, his eyes didn't match. This was proof enough to many of my contemporaries that he had come from Jupiter. (This would have made him a Jovian, which I initially thought was the technical term for a member of Bon Jovi. Bowie turned out to be from Brixton.) The point was that at that time, at that age, in that town, David Bowie was the biggest and most glamorous star imaginable and he lived in a world so far removed from ours that extra-terrestrial origin seemed a distinct possibility. The Man Who Fell to Earth he may very well have been, but he certainly hadn't crash-landed round our way. Not once was there a sighting of an androgynous alien with his balls hanging out dusting himself down at Harper Green Bowling Club or in the car park of the Jolly Crofters on Chorley Old Road.

We went to see Bowie at the Manchester Hardrock. The Hardrock was the north-west's foremost rock venue at this time and played host to all the heavyweight acts, including Led Zeppelin, Slade, Roxy Music and the Faces. However, you weren't guaranteed a great night out, as they were also in the habit of booking Uriah Heap. Originally constructed as a ten-pin bowling alley, the Hardrock building is still standing next to the Old Trafford cricket ground and is now

Mark Radcliffe

a branch of the DIY superstore B & Q. Walking round there in search of the ultimate self-tapping screw, I could swear I heard eerie reverberations from the rock'n'roll grave. Was that really just a squeaking store-room door or was it a ghostly Mick Ronson guitar line echoing round mixer taps? Was that rumble the sound of tins of paint being delivered or was it deceased Zeppelin drummer John Bonham practising paranormal paradiddles in power tools? Back then it was packed with frenzied Bowie-ites who'd paid the princely sum of £1 to stand or £1.25 to sit down. We paid £1.25 to sit (somewhere near shower curtains and accessories by my calculations), but when the lights went down we jumped up and in our excitement rushed towards the stage, which I'm fairly certain was in the space now occupied by vinyl floor coverings.

Mind you, we'd had plenty of time to get excited, because we'd been standing outside since two o'clock in the afternoon. My anticipation had actually begun early in the morning as I attempted to decide what to wear to worship at the altar of the high priest of tinsel and tat. I toyed with the idea of my sister's fun-fur bomber jacket and cork-soled platform sandals with a pair of white parallel trousers purchased from Stolen From Ivor. I flirted with the concept of my gran's Lurex twin-set in ensemble with army combat pants and baseball boots. In the end I plumped for a navy-blue Shetland wool pullover and some shapeless corduroys in that nondescript colour of green so beloved of employees of garden centres. When I come to think about it, that's pretty much all I ever wore in those days. In band photographs of that time the others are wearing leather jackets, sunglasses and Cuban-heeled boots while I appear

26

to have been mistakenly caught in frame while collecting library fines.

When David Bowie walked on stage that night and launched into 'Let's Spend the Night Together', it gave me a thrill I'd never felt before or since. He was our idol, our god, and here he was in the flesh, in the same room as us. Charging through the songs we knew note for note, he held our very dreams in his hands, and if he'd finished the gig by being tele-transported into a flying saucer hovering overhead and whisked off to Venus, we couldn't have been more amazed. In reality he was manhandled into a Ford Granada and whisked off to the Piccadilly Hotel, but nothing could puncture our euphoria. As we walked back across Manchester to get the number eight night bus to Bolton, we talked about what we'd seen and how it had defined our ideas for the new band. We were going to write our own songs, we were going to have spiky haircuts and if our mums weren't looking we were going to wear make-up.

At this juncture the Berlin Airlift was still a going concern. Guy Farringdon had been replaced by not one but two guitarists called Jeff 'Carry' Carrington and Mark 'Stocky' Sayers. This wasn't because no single musician could attempt to replicate the dexterity of the absent Eric, but because Carry and Stocky were best mates and, like buying the last two guinea-pigs in the pet-shop, it seemed a shame to break them up. This meant that on one side of the stage we now had three guitarists competing for attention, solos, and not least, considering the elephantine girth of Jerry Lumley, floor space. The logical solution to this would have been to move one of them to the other side to keep Davey Bright company, but then their lead would have been too short to plug into the single Selmer amplifier they all shared. And, in any case, standing next to the hyperactive Bright in full hair-flinging mode always carried the risk of getting showered with airborne dandruff, quite possibly interspersed with low-flying nits. As things turned out, overcrowding in the guitarists' ghetto proved short-lived as, sick of jostling for position, Jerry Lumley upped and left, taking Davey Bright with him to form a new band called Zwolff that would later play a memorable gig which the curate immortalised in the church magazine as 'certainly louder than the normal pow-wows we hold in the scout hut'. Hey, rock'n'roll.

With ranks thus depleted, desperate measures were called for and desperate measures were taken as in some desperation we recruited Michael 'Doris' Lipsey as lead vocalist. Michael, who'd adopted the nickname Doris in homage to his hero Alice Cooper, had all the things you look for in a lead singer bar one: he couldn't sing. He had a microphone, an echo unit, an acoustic guitar, an electric guitar, a great pair of cheek-bones, a meticulously dishevelled hairstyle and an impressive approximation of soporific disinterest some regarded as charisma, but he couldn't sing to save his life. We didn't worry unduly about this, however, because every time we'd performed in public so far the vocals had proved to be completely inaudible anyway, so the fact that our method front man was tone-deaf wasn't likely to become public knowledge.

The vacant bass player's position was filled by the genial Sayers, who gladly swapped instruments and stage positions if only to get away from the now sole guitarist, Jeff Carrington. In his own head, a space of considerable capacity,

Carrington's fretboard wizardry had seen off the other two pretenders to his throne. In reality, both had vacated his immediate vicinity because he was a right royal pain in the arse. In musicians' parlance, he'd developed delusions of adequacy. Sayers the bass, though, proved a revelation. He was really good at it, by which I mean he didn't attempt anything fancy but supplied a huge shuddering noise as if a rhythm had been programmed into a concrete mixer. This is just what you want in a rock band, the simple root-note stuff and not all that slapping around popularised by Mark King out of Level 42, which sounds like a wagon-load of wet fish being delivered backstage. Come the revolution, slap bass players will be straight up against that wall along with taxi-drivers, traffic wardens, tax inspectors, Fabrizio Ravanelli, Jimmy Tarbuck, John Redwood and, I would imagine, disc jockeys. No matter how brilliant you are on the bass guitar, you should understand that it is not a lead instrument. It never has been and never will be, and bassists who refuse to accept this are trouble. Look at Sting. In many ways I think the world would have been a better place if Sting and Mark Sayers had changed places. Mark is now a top accountant, and if Sting had had one ounce of his financial acumen perhaps he'd have noticed his own accountant making off with several million quid. As for Mark, well, I can't be sure he'd have saved the rain forest but I'm pretty sure he wouldn't have released *Ten Summoner's Tales*. Coincidentally they've both stayed pretty fit. Mark still plays rugby on a regular basis and Sting practises yoga with a suppleness that enables him to put his body in all kinds of unusual positions, which is no great surprise as he's had his head up his arse for years.

29

Mark Radcliffe

In rehearsals Stocky and I were shaping up to be a rhythm section which aspired to mediocrity. We were stokers in the engine room, brothers-in-arms, sultans of swing, and we had so much in common it was spooky. We were both called Mark, both went to Bolton School and both played in a band called the Berlin Airlift. I mean, statistically, what are the chances of that happening? In addition he was tall, dark, strong and handsome. I was dark, too.

Since our trip to the Bowie concert, Doris and I had been determined to inject a bit of sparkle and show business into the band, which meant that Carrington had to go. He was a reasonable player, but he had none of the Ronsonesque showmanship we were searching for. In addition he was dashingly good-looking, in a clean-cut sort of way, and was nearly as big a hit with the girls as he was with himself. What we needed was a real plank-spanking pig-ugly Flash Harry who'd write all the songs and leave the chicks, should there ever be any, to the rest of us. The only man in Bolton who fitted this description was Barry Brightwell.

Baz was a bit older than us, and so it was with some trepidation that we embarked on a fact-finding mission to Green Lane Cricket Club in order to watch him in action with Voyd, a band he'd formed with several other like-minded social misfits. Within seconds of clapping eyes on Brightwell, we knew we'd found our man. He had a Gibson SG, which he could play lightning fast not only in the usual position but also behind his head and with his tongue, though not at the same time obviously, and not in tune necessarily. He was also a real snappy dresser, sporting an electric-blue satin jacket and flared jeans he'd emblazoned with potato prints in bleach, a principle he'd also applied to his straw-like shoulder-length hair. The only slight flaw in his otherwise perfect image was that his general build made Jerry Lumley seem positively anorexic. Baz was gargantuan – one of those fat people whose flesh seems to be moving in several different directions at once under their clothes. As a result of carting round his colossal body weight, he had a puce complexion, beads of sweat permanently running down his forehead and stagnant patches of perspiration indelibly stamped under the arms of every tent-like shirt he possessed. All three of them. He was known locally as Percy Filth, and let's just say that if you were luxuriating in the jacuzzi at a health club and spotted a betrunked Barry Brightwell waddling towards you, you'd hop out smartish. This was hypothetical, of course, because he'd never been near a health club. Fortunately Doris, who knew everyone, knew Barry and attempted to convince him to throw his not inconsiderable lot in with us because we were 'young, lean, hungry and headed for the top'. In point of fact we were young, lean, hungry and headed for the chippy near Doffcocker Lodge. Brightwell looked at us with that peculiarly gormless expression of his, before wiping the froth from the corners of his mouth and slurring 'All right, brothers, I'm with you.' We cheered, slapped him on the back and embraced, which took him a bit by surprise because he only thought he'd agreed to join us for steak pudding and chips. However, once we arrived at the chip shop we pooled our bus fares home to buy him a second pie and he was putty in our hands. Which was a distinctly unpleasant sensation.

The only problem we had now was off-loading the strutting peacock Carrington, and as none of us had the bottle to confront him face to face I hatched an ingenious plan. Well, to be strictly truthful, I pinched it off Status Quo. Following the departure of drummer John Coghlan, who left to form his own band, Diesel (nice career move, John), the most appropriately named band of all time were basically a creative, if that's the right word, nucleus of Francis Rossi, Rick Parfitt and Alan Lancaster. Now at some point Rossi, the bald pony-tailed one, and Parfitt, the blond haystacked one, decided to have a break from the band. At this point Lancaster, the unpleasantly moustachioed one, packed up his bass and his Carmen heated rollers and emigrated to Australia, only to find on touchdown in Oz that his erstwhile mates had regrouped with a new bass player before he'd even cleared Heathrow airspace. I'm with Rick and Francis on this one. Anyone with big curly hair and a moustache like Alan Lancaster deserves everything they get.

So, all we had to do was call a band meeting in the boozer and announce that we were splitting up; then, as soon as Carry had strapped on his helmet (large, naturally) and pootled off on his Honda 50, the rest of us could come out from behind the bins, re-enter the pub through the snug bar and toast to future success with the glam-rock warthog Brightwell. This historic summit took place at the Halliwell Lodge Hotel and went more or less according to plan as we all told the shell-shocked Carrington we were quitting. Unfortunately a snot-flying-drunk Percy Filth arrived early and announced he was leaving the Berlin Airlift as well, despite the fact that he'd never been in it in the first place. Convincing Carry that this was obviously some raving lunatic on day release from the local mental hospital (and, believe me, there were trained psychiatrists who'd have happily gone along with that), we sank a last half of mild as the Berlin

Airlift and went our separate ways. Well, one of us did anyway. Minutes later, the rest of us were back at the bar for our first half of mild as the new band. The only thing we had to sort out was a name. Status Quo characteristically persevered with the same name, although a token change may well have been in order. As their sound has got progressively less meaty over the years, Status Quorn would have been appropriate.

Barry wanted to call the band Percy Filth, which indicated that, as egomaniacal lead guitarists went, we'd hopped out of the frying pan and into an even bigger, hotter, greasier frying pan. Doris, by now spectacularly bladdered, proclaimed that we should be Humphrey and the Wet Farts, which, I have to admit, sounds pretty good to me now. I'd been drawing a cartoon about a boy who spends so much time looking at the moon that his face turns into a reflection of it. I've no idea where this idea came from, though it may have been conceived while I was under the influence of malted milk. The boy in the story was called Billy Moon and I thought that was a great name for a band. Mark, being Mark, said, 'I'll do what Mark wants.' So we had a vote, taken admittedly while B.B. king-size was making another of his interminable toilet visits and Doris was sitting upright only with the help of a pool cue wedged between his shoulder-blades, and the name Billy Moon won the ballot unanimously: two votes cast, one abstention *in absentia*, one spoilt ballot paper.

Billy Moon rehearsed regularly in the attic of my parents' house, where I'd painted a picture of our lunar-headed mascot on the wall next to the poster of Pan's People. Pan's People were a troupe of girls who used to dance in their knickers to one song each week on *Top Of The Pops*.

33

You never knew whereabouts in the programme they would turn up, but curiously enough, no matter whose house you were watching it at, the announcement of their appearance coincided with your mate's dad entering the room whistling casually and generally feigning nonchalance. He would leave the room on three legs one song later, muttering disparaging remarks along the lines of 'Noisy rubbish, young people's pop music' and 'Bit of national service, good tune, Glenn Miller, never did me any harm', or words to that effect.

In contrast to the Berlin Airlift, the Moon *oeuvre* was made up predominantly of original material, that's to say, tunes that were self-penned, not tunes that broke exciting new musical ground. Songwriter-in-chief was the gibbering heap of lard, Percy, whose compositions, like those of many prolific songwriters, returned time and again to one central theme. With Bob Dylan it was political struggle and change, with Nick Drake it was isolation and love unrequited, with Bowie it was a passage to other worlds, with Difford and Tilbrook it was the ability of small lives to triumph over adversity, and with Barry Brightwell it was what he'd done, or would like to do, to his girlfriend Janet.

Janet was a petite, bespectacled mouse of a woman in a floral-print skirt and white nylon blouse who outwardly appeared perfectly sane. This must have been a façade, because if she'd been perfectly sane she'd never have gone out with Barry. The image of that sweaty peroxide-haired mammoth with his satin strides round his ankles leaping on top of this meek individual is one that has stayed with me down the years, and the fact that she sat in on rehearsals while the Filthster broadcast their intimate moments in song never ceased to amaze me. Some of his lyrics had a certain naïve

34

charm, such as 'She's a real humdinger – Polaroid swinger, yeh', while others had an earthier appeal. I particularly recall the heart-rending tale of the time Janet wouldn't let him into her size-eight pants because it was the wrong time of the month. To ease his frustration, he'd got paralytic in town only to find himself without bus fare walking home in the rain feeling, to quote the title of the piece, 'pissed up, pissed through and pissed off'. Now I'm not claiming he was Leonard Cohen, but these words were positively poetic compared to other gems from the Brightwell canon, such as 'Vaseline Queen', 'Gravy Down the Legs' and 'I'll Give Her One from You'. Still, we reassured ourselves that no one would hear the catalogue of depravities droned out through an inadequate PA system by the tuneless Lipsey, and safe in this knowledge set off for our début gig at the Parochial Hall.

Transport had been a perennial problem in the past, but not any more. Stocky's dad worked for a plastic-sheeting company and had promised us the use of a Ford Transit. Unfortunately, when we went to pick it up they'd put in some extra deliveries and so there was no van available. There was, however, an open-backed pick-up truck, so we borrowed that instead. Getting all the equipment on board proved no trouble at all, and Stocky was a perfectly able provisional licence-holding driver ensconced in his heated cab with the waiflike Janet in the passenger seat. For the rest of us the journey proved considerably less comfortable, not only because of the necessity of negotiating several unmade roads, but also because it was February and snowing heavily. Still, we arrived in one piece in a truck marked Dynamic

Plastics, which it strikes me now is a much better name for a band than Billy Moon. If we'd become the Dynamic Plastics we'd have had our own personalised van, just like a proper pop group.

Inside the Parochial Hall we started to position the equipment on stage. I built myself a drum riser from school desks in the time-honoured fashion of small drummers who'll take all the height they can get. Mark Sayers set about building a monumental stack of speaker cabinets to my immediate left. One of them was actually genuine and contained four speakers. The other three were entirely empty and had been constructed from sheeting offcuts at Dynamic Plastics. Still, he'd glued proper speaker cloth to the front and it all looked hugely impressive. The rocking rhinoceros Brightwell had two cabinets but, more impressively, he had three boxes of lights. When we saw these, stencilled with the legend Percy Filth, we were speechless with admiration. To be honest, we'd envisaged them being placed at regular intervals across the stage, not arranged in horseshoe formation round his bulbous, satin-clad legs, but, as he eloquently argued, they were indeed 'his bleeding lights' and he could quite reasonably put them 'where the frigging hell he liked'. Still, we had a few overhead lights left by the amateur dramatic society and our new resident electrical genius Andy Holdsworth had promised us something special for the opening sequence. Holdsworth had been recruited from the A-level physics set because, in the absence of Davey Bright, we had no one who could deal with circuitry in order to electrocute innocent bystanders. Nicknamed Menk, he had the worst case of acne I have ever seen, which caused much hilarity before gigs when, without fail, discussions about lighting would culminate in the long-suffering Holdsworth being asked, 'And have you got any spots, Menk?'

While all this was going on, our alleged singer was in the toilets applying make-up with a trowel to his sculpted features. He'd obtained a good deal of the cosmetics from his mother's dressing-table while she was at bingo, but to be fair to him he hadn't cleaned her out entirely. He wasn't that unscrupulous and, thinking first and foremost of his dear old mum, he honourably pinched the rest from Boots. After about forty-five minutes he emerged with black rings round his eyes and mouth, and red stripes down each cheek. I think he thought he looked like David Bowie, but he looked more like a coal-miner who'd lost control of a ketchup dispenser to me.

By now the hordes of fans were filling the hall and sales of Vimto were brisk. At around eight o'clock the support group Odyssey took to the stage. They were in the year below us at school and so we weren't really worried, although they did boast a precocious talent on lead guitar in the Bolan-like form of Jed Hall. Hall would many years later turn up in a renowned north-western folk group called the Westhoughton Weavers, singing such traditional favourites as 'The Lincolnshire Pig Castrator's Daughter', 'Ho down merry down with a hey nonny fol de rol doo dey' and 'Where's Me Pewter Tankard', but back then, with his cherubic curls and wraparound shades, he was every inch the trainee rock star. They also had a rich kid called Fitzsimmons, whose dad had bought him an electronic organ, which did cause us some concern because, quite simply, we hadn't got one. Within seconds of their opening number, Deep Purple's 'Black Night', it became apparent that we had a

Mark Radcliffe

slight problem on our hands: they were bloody brilliant. I'd previously only seen Barry Brightwell's face glowing a luminous red, but when Jed Hall dispatched a note-perfect solo in 'All Right Now' it drained to an ashen white. A faithful reproduction of the twenty-five-minute Pink Floyd epic 'Echoes' had us crying into our crisps, and when Hall produced a flaming guitar and smashed it during the dying chords we knew we were in big trouble. The guitar in question was only a hastily emulsioned old acoustic but the damage was done.

In the dressing-room our emotions boiled over:

'Little bastards, they're better than us.'

'I'm going to get Jed Hall and punch his lights out.'

'You know, I'd really like to go home now.'

'Has anyone seen my eye-liner pencil?'

Solemnly we made our final preparations. Baz crowbarred himself into the familiar satin and potato print, while Doris touched up the elaborate facial disguise, which to me was beginning to seem like a better idea with each passing minute. The athletic Stocky threw on a purple and black velvet jerkin, over which he hung a large, carved wooden cross, which seemed entirely appropriate given the impending crucifixion. Ever the dandy, I checked for wet patches in my corduroys before pulling off my Shetland pullover to reveal a nicely pressed check shirt. Suitably attired, we took the short walk from death row and went up the stairs to the gallows.

To create the maximum amount of tension and excitement, we took the stage in total darkness, which proved a costly mistake for our lanky and spectacularly cidered front man as he immediately cracked his head on a steel girder, knocking himself practically senseless and rearranging the meticulously applied make-up on his forehead into a kind a psychedelic smudge. As I sat centre stage in pitch-blackness wondering why the hell I was doing this – a thought that would cross my mind at regular intervals over the coming years – a loud, resonant farting noise emanated from the abyss stage left. Fortunately, this proved to be Stocky plugging his bass in. Unfortunately, the loud, resonant farting noise which almost immediately followed from the black hole stage right proved to be Percy Filth copiously breaking wind. Of course, we'd been blown away by Bowie making his entrance through a fog of dry ice, and one day hoped to launch into our first number amid swirling clouds of noxious gas, but not like this. The brimstone whiff of hell's intestine did nothing to lift our spirits as Mark kick-started his bass to create the low rumble from which Led Zeppelin's 'Livin' Lovin' Maid' would eventually materialise. This was the prearranged cue for Menk the Spot to dramatically unleash his lighting arsenal and bathe the stage in an atmospheric glow. He'd been instructed to pay particular attention to our stunning backdrop, which featured a three-foot-high cardboard cut-out of our mascot, Billy Moon. I'd been working on this for weeks with scissors, silver paint and several Pritt sticks, and was confident that it now looked like an entranced, unbearably cute little round-faced cartoon character who'd absorbed mystical lunar qualities. Looking at the photos now, it looks more like a dwarf who's been hit with a frying pan while suffering from a severe case of the mumps. Mercifully, hardly anyone saw it, in any case, as the full mind-blowing Menk Holdsworth optical experience proved to consist of waiting for the first power chord, and then, bang on three seconds after the cue, throwing an impressive-looking lever to activate a standard sixty-watt household bulb hanging from a flex over the stage. Kiss at Castle Donnington it wasn't.

Incredibly, despite the debilitating nerves, Stocky and Percy executed the 'Livin' Lovin' Maid' riffs with admirable precision, though sadly not at the same time. To this day I have no idea how they managed it, but from the first flat line to escape from the mouth of the man in the mascara mask they were playing completely different sections of the song. It's at times like this that you're thankful for being the drummer. Sitting at the back out of range of all but the hardest-thrown Tizer cans, you simply put your head down and keep clobbering away until they've sorted themselves out or the song has finished. Whichever is the most unexpected.

For the lead singer, the focus of all the attention down the front, the situation was little short of catastrophic. Already reeling from a potent combination of concussion and Strongbow, the gaily painted Doris was faced with a choice of which of his henchmen to follow. In no fit state to make such a choice, he settled instead for ploughing on in his adenoidal drone while shooting nervous glances left and right. His face, illuminated sporadically by a light show that was more public lavatory than Brixton Academy, resembled a giant ladybird fluttering backwards and forwards across the stage in some distress. Somehow we managed to reach the end of the Zeppelin classic within ten seconds of each other, and if Jimmy Page, Robert Plant and John Paul Jones had been dead, they'd have been turning in their graves with John Bonham. Having triumphantly failed to please the crowd with the crowd-pleasing rock standard opener, we then launched into a brace of numbers from the forthcoming concept album *Things to Make and Do When You Get in Janet's Pants*. To say the audience's reaction remained muted during 'Vaseline Queen', 'Polaroid Swinger' and 'Gravy Down the Legs' is a bit like calling the critical response to Duran Duran's 1995 cover versions album *Thank You* mixed, but we put this down to lack of familiarity with the material. Facing the same look of mass bafflement at future gigs, this was an excuse we'd never have the luxury of using again.

By this time the lank-haired blob to my right, who some of the audience evidently thought was the wrestler Giant Haystacks caught up in a freak double-booking accident, decided it was time to perform his party piece, or, if you prefer, play his joker. During the instrumental break of 'Pissed Up, Pissed Through and Pissed Off', he played a reasonable solo in the first position, a ropey solo behind his head and a rip-roaringly rotten solo with his tongue. God knows why, but the audience loved it. As far as I was concerned, the technique sounded bloody awful even when Jimi Hendrix did it, but at least he was the wiry sex-god hip-priest of his age. When performed by a bleached beached whale from Bromley Cross, it seemed an entertainment-free zone to me, but there's no accounting for taste. As I sat there, pummelling out some indeterminate and imprecise rhythm, watching Barry drooling on to his pick-ups, I consoled myself that even though things were bad, at least I'd never come near the end of his salivating tongue. How Janet got through the day I really couldn't imagine. As the song shuddered to a halt we heard a strange noise that sounded vaguely familiar, although it took us a few seconds to recognise it as applause. During this unexpected interlude Percy pulled a rancid towel from his duffle bag and proceeded to wipe the spittle from his strings, and I remember thinking that if it's true that all good guitars have their own personality then this one must be thoroughly cheesed off. I presume he eventually sold the SG on, and I can only hope he did so with a health warning; then at least the new owner could get it steam-cleaned. Still, we had public approval to propel us onwards now and, not wanting to take any chances, we hurried through Golden Earring's 'Radar Love', the inevitable 'Johnny B. Goode' and an uncharacteristically sensitive Brightwell ballad built around the poignant chorus couplet 'Love is so fickle, Let me touch you, let me tickle'. Oddly, this seemed to strike a chord with young lovers in the audience, who snogged each other blind while Baz demonstrated how he could make his guitar gently weep, while simultaneously adopting strange facial expressions which appeared to indicate extreme digestive difficulties.

As the song put itself out of its misery there was a smattering of applause, but most of those present, having discovered the joys of sticking their tongues down each others' throats, remained more interested in experiencing first-hand heavy petting than third-rate heavy metal. Having thus snatched defeat from the jaws of victory, we lumbered into our last song, the anthemic 'I'll Give Her One from You', during which the irrepressible Menk Holdsworth unleashed his final inventive masterstroke by switching on an anglepoise lamp behind Mark Sayers' speakers in an attempt to give the stage a ghostly back-lit radiance. All this actually achieved was to demonstrate that the cabinets were entirely empty and were there only as a tawdry bit of set dressing. As if being caught red-handed in possession of the bogus bass bins wasn't enough, we had to endure further indignity before reaching the sanctity of the dressing-room. In a real stroke of bad luck the sound engineer Harold, who'd come on hire with the PA system, had proved to be more than capable and had succeeded in making the vocals audible. Had he been a friend of ours, he would have safely buried them out of harm's way, but instead the bewildered parents who'd arrived to pick up their slobbering offspring gathered at the rear of the hall to witness an off-key beanpole in face paint shriek the memorable lines:

I wanna rock it to her,
I wanna sock it to her,
If it's the last thing that I do,
I'll give her one from you.

Worse still, one of the gobsmacked dads turned out to be my English teacher, Mr Corcoran, whose face crumbled at witnessing this flagrant misuse of his beloved native tongue. As he commented in poetry class the next week, the lyrical style of Billy Moon had very little in common with that of Gerard Manley Hopkins.

It was with a palpable sense of relief, then, that we reached our final pile-driver chord, during the sustain of which I slashed the backdrop to shreds with a brass fencing sword I'd taken down from over Auntie Mary's fireplace. What a showman. What a tosser. With an exhibition of dextrous handling that wouldn't have been out of place on *One Man and His Dog*, the remnants of the crowd were then herded out of the fire exit by their exasperated guardians with only slightly less speed than that achieved by the band fleeing the stage. To bring the evening full circle, and anticipating your disbelief – I promise this is true – the desolate Lipsey smacked his painted-by-numbers face into the same cross-beam he'd head-butted before we'd even played a note.

We didn't do an encore, because Barry had broken a string and didn't want to use another one.

We played a few more times after that but, to be honest we were, even at that early stage, pulling in different directions, often during the same song. I think we all realised that the writing was on the wall. The wall in question ran down Dobson Road next to the school playing fields and the writing daubed on it read: 'Billy Moon are shit'.

Eventually, big Baz left to investigate the world of cabaret. We last saw him at Moor Lane bus station with an acoustic guitar wrapped in a floral duvet cover saying he was off to an audition for *Opportunity Knocks* (it didn't), while Doris left to investigate the world of mind-bending narcotics. Mark and I, like two First World War veterans who'd bonded in the trenches through their shared traumatic experiences, decided we'd stay together and find another band.

It could only get better.

3

Zoot Suit and the Zeroids

Amazingly, it did get better when we formed Zoot Suit and the Zeroids. The genesis of the band has uncanny parallels with the formation of that other revered heavy-blues combo Led Zeppelin, and in fact seasoned Zep watchers will often wistfully mention the Zeroids in the same breath. Like Led Zeppelin, the Zeroids had a Z in it, but there was even more to it than that. Both bands represented a coming together of two disparate duos. Jimmy Page and John Paul Jones were already established musicians, having played with such household names as the Yardbirds, Donovan and P.J. Proby when they recruited unknowns Robert Plant and John Bonham from the heavy-metal heartland known as the Black Country in homage to the local demon overlords Black Sabbath. With spooky similarity, Stig Burgess and Paul Hemingway were veterans not only of Cairo, who played a memorable set for the Girl Guides at Woodlands, but also of the seminal Macaris Lives Big Band in a line-up completed, as you probably already know, by Spider and Earl. To say Stocky and I were unknowns wouldn't be strictly accurate, because the name Billy Moon had been widely circulated, often with a public health warning, but we were certainly aware we'd moved up a league. From the Beazer Homes to the GM Vauxhall Conference.

Stig was a revelation to us. He knew songs the like of which we'd never heard: Otis Redding songs, Jonathan Richman songs, Gram Parsons songs, Ry Cooder songs. He'd even got a few of his own, which, like a lot of J.J. Cale's compositions, appeared simplistic and almost half-hearted, but which took on a timeless quality when he played them, as if they could have been written at any time during the last fifty years. They had throwaway titles like 'Good Time Man' or 'Running Down the Road', and he'd strum the three rudimentary chords on his natural Fender Telecaster while mumbling the lyrics with his eyes closed. In his floppy cap, straggly hair and bushy beard he had modelled himself on Lowell George. If you don't know who Lowell George is, then get hold of an album by the late lamented American rolling-boogie band Little Feat and look at the photograph of the players. The one who looks like a latter-day George Best after a three-day binge is the revered slide guitarist, songwriter and singer Lowell George. Lowell was known in his day as a bit of a hellraiser in that he liked women, drugs and food in formidable quantities and, I daresay, even enjoyed the odd shandy, and quite possibly a glass of sweet sherry on special occasions. How these rock stars manage to satisfy these outrageous appetites and live to a ripe old age is a mystery to me. Sadly, it was also a mystery to Lowell George, who died in 1979 at the age of thirty-four.

Relatively tame in comparison, Stig's level of debauchery was restricted to a regular fix of Watney's dark mild, but he desperately wanted to be American. In his mind, I'm sure he saw himself as a dust-bowl balladeer of the late forties, cruising the lost highways in a battered pick-up truck wearing gasoline-splattered dungarees. In reality he was a lab technician in his late twenties cruising Chorley New Road in a battered Vauxhall Viva. He did have the dungarees, though. I met Stig through a mate of mine called Joe Goulden, who I'd arranged to hook up with in town to visit the wine lodge on Bradshawgate, which gleefully added to its legitimate income by selling tumblers of warm Australian wine to underage drinkers. Joe was heavily involved with the Venture Scouts and, en route to the penny blob shebeen, had to drop in at a meeting about the next trek camp at the Swan. This didn't seem a very ambitious trek camp destination to me. The Swan was only on the corner of Churchgate, for Christ's sake. Anyway, after a couple of pints and several bags of pork scratchings, Stig and I got chatting about music and he was raving on about this new American genius called Bruce Springsteen, who was going to be the biggest star in the world. I took this with a pinch of salt, safe in the knowledge that whoever this Springclean divot was, he'd never be as big as the Strawbs.

During the course of the conversation Stig mentioned that he was a singer and guitarist and had a mate who'd played sax with him in the recently disbanded Macaris Lives, thus instigating a search for a new rhythm section. It was one of those historic meetings which really ought to be commemorated with a plaque. Like Rolls meeting Royce, like Livingstone meeting Stanley, like, at the risk of getting carried away, Little meeting Large, it was obvious that fate had drawn us together that night. Stig introduced me to his sax-playing mate Paul Hemingway, who was another prime

mover in the Venture Scouts. The Venture Scouts were a
faction I knew very little about, because I never made it
beyond the Wolf Cubs. In fact I only lasted there about a
month, because my mum wouldn't buy me the green jersey
until she was sure I was 'going to fit in'. Being the only kid
in the scout hut in a Fair Isle cardigan, there wasn't much
chance of that.

Paul Hemingway was the only bloke in Bolton who had a
saxophone and had mastered all the rock'n'roll techniques
associated with it. These are, in ascending order of impor-
tance, making it go honk, making it go squeak and swinging
it from side to side while winking at girls in the audience.
Every song we played was embellished during the chorus with
a succession of bowel-loosening honks interspersed with the
squawking sound of an asphyxiated iguana in its death throes.
If confronted by the appearance of these rogue reed splits,
sax players are apt to get defensive and say 'I meant to do
that, you musical philistine', and throw several more in the
next time round just to prove it was intentional. We gave up
discussing it with him in the end, but it always struck me as
odd that if he meant to make that noise, then how come it
always happened in a different place, and why did he look
as startled as the rest of us? Like his guitar-toting compadre,
Paul appeared to have modelled himself on a famous exponent
of his chosen instrument, but whereas Stig's role model was
a respected blues icon, Paul's was the saxophonist off *The
Muppets*. When it came to developing a physical resemblance
to this puppet idol, Paul had a head start, because he looked
like him to begin with, and once his protuberant hooter and
bulging eyes had been topped with a battered fedora, it
wouldn't have been a surprise, except possibly to his wife

Jennifer, to sneak round the back and find Jim Henson's hand up his arse.

Eventually Zoot Suit and the Zeroids would rehearse up a set of soul and blues and country that would come to be met with polite applause rather than the bewildered stares that Stocky and I were used to. We'd play gigs attended by up to fifty at Pip's Night-spot, Rivington Barn and even the Cypress Tavern in Manchester, where the lack of stage lighting resulted in an eleventh-hour dash back to Bolton in the Viva to borrow two desk lamps. Years later, Talking Heads performed at the Free Trade Hall with a stage lit only by white light, and I often wonder if David Byrne had seen the Zeroids at the Cypress Tavern that night. It's quite possible that he might have been ploughing a lonely furrow through the unfamiliar city streets, drawn inexorably towards the sign that read: 'Tonight: Vodka Fifty Pence A Shot plus live band'. However, this was all in the future, as both Stig and Paul were off to Marrakesh on the Venture Scouts' trek camp, where they would walk several hundred miles with army surplus stoves on their backs and attempt to live on ten pence a week. All we knew at this stage was that the four of us were going to be in a band together. We had no idea what it was going to sound like until several months later, when we would go to a gig that would knock us completely off our feet. In the meantime, it was all on hold while they spent the summer getting heat-stroke digging latrines in North Africa, and Stocky and I lazed around my bedroom contemplating the colour of Pippa Johnson's pants.

By this time Mark and I had become sixth formers, which meant that we'd undergone several major changes of life.

For a kick-off, we were allowed to wear our own clothes to school. You were still obliged to dress smartly, but you were freed from the shackles of uniform. I was particularly proud of my brown three-piece, wide-lapelled, improbably flared suit, in which I felt the essence of cool right up to spilling a jug of parsley sauce down it in the dining-hall.

We were also transforming physically. With a good stacked heel, I was now very nearly as tall as some of the girls I was trying to get off with.

Mentally I was maturing as well. I no longer felt the need to bait my sister on a daily basis. Sometimes we would go for as long as two or three days without a sporadic outbreak of mindless violence. I still ignored my little brother for weeks at a time, not so much because he was 'just a nipper' but because he was so much better at football than I was. He had better hair, too. He was five years younger than me and yet he had thick, shiny gorgonesque curls down to his shoulders. I was supposed to be the trainee hippy in that household!

What I had perfected was a teenage expertise in laziness. That summer I convinced myself that I wasn't just being bone idle, but that like many musicians and thespians I was 'resting' between engagements. A plumber or decorator would be more likely to describe this situation as 'unemployment', but in performing circles it's known as 'resting' and you can't help wishing that the members of Iron Maiden had rested a good deal longer.

While I was euphemistically 'resting', I immersed myself in buying vast quantities of LPs, which I took up to my bedroom to listen to intently while studying the sleeve notes obsessively. It wasn't just the lyrics I memorised, it was crucial information like the studio where it had been recorded (often Rockfield), the name of the tape op (regularly Alan Parsons) and the identity of the cover artist (just about always Roger Dean). This addiction to the accumulation of anorak information plagues me even now. I'm the bloke who sits in the cinema and watches the film right through to the end of the credits, just to make sure it was recorded in Dolby stereo. (Incidentally, I don't think the boffins who invented Dolby stereo are all that industrious. Dolby B and Dolby C have been around years now, and there's still no sign of them coming up with Dolby D.)

When buying a record, it was vital to remember that not only was no one else allowed to have heard of it, but there had to be a good chance that your mum and dad would hate it. The obscurity factor was crucial in terms of enhancing your personal credibility. Often I would purchase albums by bands I'd never even heard of myself, just for the thrill of walking into the sixth-form common room with Amazing Blondel's *Fantasia Lindum* under my arm. Of course, this was a risky purchasing policy because for every Flying Burrito Brothers you had to go through a ruck of Horslips or Blodwyn Pigs or Tonto's Expanding Headbands. This put something of a drain on my meagre finances, but it was worth it for the heart-stopping moments when you bought a record because you liked the sleeve, and when you put it on discovered that this Alex Harvey bloke had, in *Next*, made one of the truly great albums. It sounds ridiculous, but I'm sure long-standing fans of the Velvet Underground, U2, REM and Oasis feel the same way. That it was somehow better when it was secret.

The parental annoyance factor was equally important. It is one of those unbreakable rules of adolescence that you must develop a taste for whatever kind of music your parents like the least. If your mum and dad like Sepultura, go out and buy Suzanne Vega; if your mum and dad like the Beautiful South, go out and buy Public Enemy; and if your mum and dad like Phil Collins, leave home immediately. From trad jazz, through rock'n'roll, heavy metal, progressive rock, punk, rap and house, teen music has always been something your parents hated. As a pimply youth I remember thinking how dreadful it was when I went round to my mate Nicky Holt's house to listen to records and his dad, Trevor, would come into the room and profess to be taking an interest. Standing in the corner with his neatly trimmed moustache, bifocals and cardigan with leatherette panels, he'd tap his right Hush Puppy and say things like 'Yes, very jaunty, King Crimson really are a proficient beat group, aren't they, boys?' or 'I must say, this Pink Floyd fellow has a resonant singing tone and that Jethro Tull chap is a very accomplished flautist.'

When your dad likes your record collection it's time to move on. Even if it means Marilyn Manson. I spent years following acts I wasn't that bothered about just because it annoyed my mum. When Arthur Brown appeared on *Top of the Pops* singing 'Fire' in streaked face paint, a silk kimono and a flaming head-dress, I really couldn't have cared less until my mum said, 'Well, look at that idiot in a ladies' blouse with his balaclava on fire and he hasn't even washed his face.' After that, I'd have followed him anywhere. Even, on one occasion, Hebden Bridge. The point is that every era of teen culture has its defining musical movement, which you only fully understand if you're the right age and go to the right clubs. When I hear the latest techno releases and say 'Well, where's the tune in that, then?' I get looked at like I'm a silly old tosser. In truth, I get looked at that way relatively often, and not just in relation to music, but why should I relate to techno? I'm a forty-year-old father who these days finds most pub juke-boxes a tad intrusive, and if I understand techno then techno's got it wrong. And anyway, if I pretended to like techno then I'd have turned into Trevor Holt, and I'm not ready for that cardigan just yet, although a pair of comfortable Hush Puppies does look increasingly tempting.

The live gigs we went to took place almost exclusively at Bolton Institute of Technology, a sprawl of charmless glass and concrete obelisks on a patch of scrubland between dual carriageways. A large proportion of the inmates were the kind of students who were too thick to go to polytechnic and too lazy to sign on. Instead they led a peculiar twilight existence tramping around the back streets of Bolton with unkempt beards, trying to summon up the concentration to roll another fag. They were the kind of people who considered expending energy was distinctly uncool and had to think long and hard about whether they could be bothered to remove their trousers before evacuating their bowels. I'm quite sure some of them perfected acute constipation to save themselves the effort of wiping their arses.

Intermingled with the bobble-hatted undead were desperately keen clean-cut innocents from the Middle East whose wealthy guardians had been seduced into coughing up extortionate fees to send their precious offspring to what the prospectus implied was one of our finest Ivy League institutions. Once there, our foreign friends would hone their linguistic skills while discussing ergonomics in the windswept modernist piazzas with the cream of England's public-school intelligentsia. Or so their parents thought. During recess, accounting for no more than thirty-six weeks of the year, they were expected to return home intellectually sharper with an intimate knowledge of British business practice, ready to revolutionise the running of the family empire. In reality they got back two stone heavier with an intricate knowledge of joint rolling, ready to sleep for six weeks.

Every Saturday night there was a band on at the BIT union bar. In theory this was open to students only, but as security was undertaken by campus inhabitants who were horizontal by eight-thirty, it wasn't difficult to slip in. Being schoolboys, Stocky and I might have looked incongruous with our neat haircuts and chain-store slacks, but the yetis on the door probably assumed we'd come from Saudi Arabia to study metallurgy. Once through the security cordon, you entered a large room filled with luminescent orange foam furniture on which hirsute zombies in brushed denim performed tonsillectomies on each other, while paralysis-inducing strobe lights blinked along to Hendrix's 'Purple Haze'. Brilliant.

On a good day the rugby scrum at the beer pumps could be negotiated in as little as thirty-five minutes. The principal reason for the delay was not that the cigarette-burn-peppered melamine bar itself was the length of the counter in a down-at-heel toffee shop, but that it was staffed entirely by volunteers from the student populace. Reaching the front of the queue, you could swear you'd arrived in a world devised by Tolkien where hairy little trolls in woollen bonnets sloped around in a somnambulant shuffle. On a hot night it'd be touch and go whether you'd get your pint before it evaporated. Payment took the form of a token feudal exchange of coinage, but goods, services or the promise of a big tonguey snog later seemed to do nicely as well. God knows who underwrote the potentially crippling losses, but I've a strong suspicion that it was the parents of those Saudi Arabian guys who received a letter from the principal assuring them that it was absolutely the norm for union subscriptions to run into the thousands.

Having successfully obtained two bottles of Newcastle Amber each, we would then step carefully over tie-dyed, frizzy-haired couples who'd decided that copulation was a sport best undertaken on a crowded dance floor, to sit cross-legged in front of the stage and wait for the band. I've always found sitting cross-legged distinctly uncomfortable, but no self-respecting trainee student was allowed to sit any other way. One thing was for sure, if I'd unfolded a small camping stool I'd have stood even less chance of swapping spit with that drug-addled, ethnic-shirted, afro-haired biochemist from Luton. Dennis, I think he was called.

There was a different band on every week, but the casual observer would have been hard pushed to notice the difference, such were the similarities between them. Admittedly they all had different names, which would normally have been a dead giveaway, but there were people in that building whose state of mind was so fragile that remembering who they'd seen last week was a mental peak they were incapable of scaling. I can recall witnessing such legends as Gong, Aange, Amon Duul, Magma, Fruup, Hatfield And The North and, of course, the mighty Hawkwind. Wholly disparate groups, they shared many common elements. For a start, the members of each band all seemed to live together on some semi-derelict ramshackle pig farm in Belgium, despite which they all dressed in the manner of the Pied Piper of Hamelin newly installed as a U-boat captain. Additionally, each line-up contained at least nine people, one of whom would always be bald, another of whom would play an instrument you wouldn't expect to find in a rock band, for instance a cor anglais, alpine horn or sackbut, and yet another would weave around the stage in a catatonic trance, evidently interpreting the vibes in mime and movement.

Week after week we trooped along there to see the same old pageant played out on a concert platform bathed in the glow of oil wheels. Another prerequisite for any serious space-rock co-operative, the oil wheel was a revolving disc of multicoloured goo through which a beam of light was directed at the turn. The same effect can be achieved by vomiting into a slide projector. A normal evening's events would start with the oil wheels flickering into life as a variety of squeaks, farts and an enema-inducing bass rumble emanated from the speakers. For a while it would be unclear if the band had started or if demolition work was being undertaken near by. After several minutes a character resembling Baldrick in a flying helmet holding a euphonium would waddle up to the microphone and say, 'Hi, we're Icarus's Ballbag from the pig fields of Benelux, and this is our oratorio for abused Mother Earth – it's called "Psycho Sacrilege Sinfonietta".' At this point there would be a mass awakening of hibernating hairies who would rush towards the stage to move their arms like tree branches in a stiff breeze. This made a swift return to the bar extremely hazardous.

Of all the bands in this illustrious company, by far the most revered were Hawkwind. They portrayed themselves as hippy-dippy space cowboys travelling to distant galaxies in search of new worlds which were free from capitalist greed and abundantly blessed with magic mushrooms. Well, that all sounds perfectly reasonable, but imagine future generations spending myriad light years traversing the cosmos to touch down on a lush, verdant planet only to find that Hawkwind had got there first. It would be like Hillary and Tensing hauling themselves to the peak of Everest only to find two pensioners in collapsible chairs sitting alongside a dormobile. Nevertheless, if we're talking about the ingredients a band needed to impress the teenage impressionable, then Hawkwind had them all. They not only had a bald bloke, Del Dettmar, and an unusual instrument, something called an audio generator manned by one Dik Mik, but they also had the greatest dancer of them all in Stacia. Stacia was a woman from Exeter who impressed us enormously with her elaborate make-up, exotic costumes and expressive choreography. What impressed us even more enormously, though, were her enormous and impressively bare breasts, which she jiggled about during the performance. It was a tonic and no mistake. As if all this wasn't enough to command the utmost awe and respect, they had a resident poet in the late Robert Calvert, a sci-fi guru in Michael Moorcock, a genuine rock god in commander Dave Brock and a crater-faced grebo rock'n'roll icon in legendary bass player, Lemmy.

One of the other things that Stocky and I thought was wonderful about Hawkwind was the amount of equipment they had. As far as we were concerned, the more gear a band brought with them, the better they were. Hawkwind had a kit with double bass drums, synthesisers with patch bays like antiquated telephone exchanges, amplifiers the size of Welsh dressers and breasts the size of space hoppers. They were the biggest, barest, baldest, barmiest, beardiest band to bowl over BIT since Black Oak Arkansas. We'd seen the future and that future was space rock. With me and Mark and Stig and Paul in place already, despite the fact that the other two were several hundred miles away cooking dead rats in pond water and had once described Hawkwind as 'the biggest bunch of shitheads in the world', we just needed a violinist, a bassoonist, a projectionist, a pianist who'd be prepared to have his head shaved and a female gymnast with a burgeoning interest in naturism, and we'd be in business. I had Pippa Johnson pencilled in as the exotic dancer, but as the contents of her bra were still a promised land I'd yet to visit, the idea that she was going to put her bosom on display in the back room of the Black Dog at Belmont and swing it in the general direction of the mild-sipping regulars while the rest of us indulged in a bout of extended rifferama seemed optimistic, to say the least. As things turned out, she never got the opportunity. If I had become her Svengali, her life might have turned out very differently and instead of living with a captain of European industry in a period house in Hertfordshire she could well have had a regular lap-dancing engagement at Tonge Moor Labour Club. The reason her career in showbusiness remained unexplored and our cohort of cosmic crusties unrecruited was from Canvey Island in Essex and it was called Dr Feelgood.

Stig and Paul had returned from their desert camp and had suggested going to see this band called Dr Feelgood who were appearing on Saturday at BIT. We'd never heard of them, which was no great surprise, because we'd never heard of most of the bands who appeared there. In fact I'm convinced some of those crumhorn-wielding Flemish swineherds were just blokes from Bury who hadn't quite mastered English but had realised that if you called yourselves Undulating Camembert or Captain Nemo's Heaving Buttocks or Ogg and said you were big in Luxemburg, you'd get a well-paid gig and a good night out. Of course, pulling this off hinged on pretending you were Belgian, which is a bridge too far for most people – but acid is a very potent drug.

Arriving in front of the familiar stage that night, our first reaction was one of crushing disappointment. The great gods Hawkwind had taught us to gauge the worth of a band by the tonnage of their equipment, which had to mean that this Dr Feelgood were the worst group in the world, not counting the ones we'd been in. Centre stage was a white drum-kit consisting of four drums and three cymbals. Pathetic. Where were the gongs, the glockenspiels and the goatskin timpani? Either side of this feeble display were single amplifiers the size of an average suitcase. But where were the Marshall four-by-twelves and the Ampeg bass bins and the rotating Leslie cabinets? This lot were obviously rubbish. Even the industrial skip-sized PA has been replaced with four paltry-looking Wem columns. We seriously considered the possibility of going home before the band even started, so convinced were we that the impending show was going to be rotten.

When the four members of the band walked on stage, we knew our preconceptions were right. Instead of the usual formation of crushed-velvet robed druids moving slowly across the stage, we were confronted with two wiry geezers sporting short haircuts evidently styled with Spear & Jackson hedge clippers and suits which appeared to have been cut for two even wirier geezers sometime in the 1950s. It was a look we'd seen before, but only on psychiatric patients or junior bank clerks. Behind them, on bass and drums, were two burly blokes in bad sports jackets who resembled a pair of ageing boozers who'd been recruited from the local taproom, which, we later discovered, is exactly what they were.

From the very first song it became apparent that our lives had changed and very much for the better, at that. The two thickset bricklayers at the back, John B. Sparks on bass and inexcusable moustache, and the aptly named Big Figure on drums and unpleasantly pomaded hair, set off at a fierce pace which belied their corpulence. Up front, the singer Lee Brilleaux began to twitch as he forced out his gravelly bark while the psychotic guitarist Wilko Johnson charged with faltering footsteps across the stage like an inebriated navvy being chased by marauding skinheads. We'd never heard anything like it before. Short, punchy, soulful songs performed at a hundred miles an hour by four twitching care-in-the-community candidates. The energy they put into their performance was a real awakening for us, which wasn't altogether surprising as with most of the bands we saw it was difficult to tell whether the members were asleep or not, especially the ones on the *chaises longues*. With the Feelgoods, as we soon came to lovingly refer to them, it was like someone had turned on a single brilliant white bulb which cut through all the oil wheels we'd ever seen. The songs they played were rhythm and blues standards like 'Route 66' and 'Walking the Dog', interspersed with Johnson originals such as 'She Does It Right' and 'Roxette'. I'd never heard any of them before, but they all sounded like classics to me. They played for what I estimate to have been about forty-five minutes, which for Hawkwind meant two songs, or possibly three of their snappier ones. In that time they rattled through a good fifteen numbers, during which we remained transfixed. After the gig it became clear that space rock had been jettisoned for ever:

'Jesus Christ, Stig, that was the greatest thing I've ever seen.'

'Dead right. Shall we get some skinny suits tomorrow?'

The following Saturday, Stig and I met in town and as well as buying outfits from Oxfam we got Dr Feelgood's début mono album, *Down by the Jetty*, and set about a wholesale pilfering of the sound to kick-start Zoot Suit and the Zeroids. To say they were a profound influence on us would be less truthful than saying we nicked their whole act, not only because we loved the music but because we recognised that being four ungainly misfits with ill-fitting suits and mental-institution regulation hairdos was a pretty realistic aspiration.

Listening to the taut, scratchy sound of that record now, it's hard to imagine what an impact it had on young impressionable ears tuned entirely to progressive rock. For the first time, we realised that a two-minute staccato burst of speed-spiked soul communicated more emotion than a pomp concept trilogy ever could. Dr Feelgood cured our addiction to prog, and music was never the same for us again. That album came out in 1975. The following summer we started to hear about this thing called 'punk rock', and that's a sequence of events that is by no means unconnected, to my mind.

One Saturday morning in 1994 I picked up the newspapers from behind the door to find the front pages dominated by the tragic suicide of Nirvana's Kurt Cobain. Shocking though that event was, the same editions contained news of another untimely rock'n'roll demise which, though it appeared several pages away from the leader columns and banner headlines, hit me much harder. Lee Brilleaux had succumbed to lymphoma, aged forty-one. I'd like to say here and now that Lee was a hero to me, and every band I've ever been in since that night at BIT has been in some way influenced by Dr Feelgood, which out of all the testimonies his family, friends and fans have heard must rank as easily the least important.

Towards the end of 1976, Zoot Suit and the Zeroids split up. The 'build 'em up, knock 'em down' attitude of the music press is well known, and their callous lack of interest in the fragmentation of the Zeroids does their tarnished reputation no good at all. With a few favourable column inches we could have been the best-loved British sax-based R'n'B act since the Extremely Average White Band. That those plaudits never came is to the eternal disgrace of the staff of the *New Musical Express*, and I just hope they can live with themselves amid the detritus of shattered schoolboy dreams. In their defence, it could be argued that they couldn't very well be held responsible for the break up of a band they'd never heard of. What a pathetic line of defence that is, Your Honour. If those seasoned hacks failed to keep their ears to the ground to anticipate vibrant new cultural forces, then that's tantamount to admitting gross negligence in my book (i.e., this one). In any case, I find it hard to believe that our concerted publicity campaign could have gone unnoticed even by the most blinkered of rock journalists. For our gig at the Crown in Horwich we not only put posters up in the Venture Scouts' hut and the sixth-form common room, but also made sure it was in the classified adverts section of the parish magazine. If lazy features editors at *Melody Maker* can't be bothered to check out rival publications, then the future for new music in this country looks as bleak as it did for the disillusioned Zeroids, whose bleak future was thankfully already behind them at that point.

There are those who will say that as the era of punk dawned the voice of music journalism was steeped in a cynical polemic which has been diluted over the years, and that our combo would provoke much greater interest if it were plying its trade today. I think I can disprove this with some authority. During the exhaustive research for this book, I phoned the *NME* and asked to be put through to the news desk. After first having to hold for the best part of forty-five seconds, I was connected to a female member of staff who adopted a rather snooty tone:

'Yes, sir, how may I help you?'

Honestly, the arrogance of these people. Why did she assume she was in a position to help me when in fact it was I, armed with a hot rock of a story that her paltry publication had thus far failed to report, who was much better placed to help her. Still, being a reasonable man I kept my cool:

'I've got an exclusive for your news page, you toffee-nosed cow.'

Redial buttons are a wonderful feature of the contemporary telephone, don't you think? This time my call was dealt with by a brusque sort of bloke who simply barked 'News desk' when he answered. I mean, really, if these people are incapable of adopting a code of simple manners and politeness, then they should sod off and crawl up a dead bear's bum. Anyway, cordial as ever, I persevered:

'I've got an exclusive for your news page, cock.'

'Go on, then.'
'Zoot Suit and the Zeroids have split up.'
'Who?'
'Zoot Suit and the Zeroids.'
'I've never heard of them. When was this?'
'1976.'
'Who is this?'

Isn't it marvellous that by putting the digits 141 in front of your call you can conceal the number from which you're dialling? What a triumph for our modern telecommunications network. British Telecom, I salute you in your diligence. What a pity we can't pat the music press on the back in the same way. They are as rude, arrogant, aloof and badly informed as ever, and are probably the offspring of cockney barrow boys who sell Tower of London snowstorms at extortionate prices to Japanese tourists who've stumbled on one of these East End street markets in the Port O'Bellow Road. It gives me no great pleasure to dish the dirt like this, but I've given them several chances to get their act together and they've failed every time. What's more, I think the scientific study I've mounted, the findings of which I've meticulously documented above, will prove that these criticisms are based on genuine empirical evidence and not the bitter ramblings of a rock'n'roll nobody.

Apart from the vicious disregard shown by the press, there were a number of other factors at play in the splintering of the Zeroids. Stocky was still without an amplifier to call his own. We forgave him on the grounds of his professed poverty, but when he passed his driving test and turned up in a newly purchased powder-blue Triumph Spitfire we began to question his commitment. The Triumph Spitfire was a car for posers operating on a tight budget in as much as it looked like a sports car but was considerably cheaper than the real thing. The powder-blue Triumph Spitfire was a car for posers operating on a tight budget who had no sense of pride or style and were most probably colour-blind as well. I think what hurt us most about this transition from boss bassman to boy racer was the wholly inappropriate nature of his chosen vehicle. Transport to gigs was always a problem and, in the unlikely event of him ever getting his own equipment, there was no way it was ever going to fit in his toytown dragster without first removing the roof, seats and driver.

In addition, he began to talk of his ambition to become an accountant, which as far as we were concerned was about as uncool as it was possible to be. If you were in a band, you didn't worry about money. After the music, you cogitated on the mythical rock'n'roll lifestyle of fast cars (which ruled out Triumph Spitfires), private planes, vintage champagne, loose women and loose bowels. Of course, most young rockers who embark on this course find themselves eighteen months later back in their council flats in Dagenham with nothing to show for the platinum sales of their début album in the States but an irksome stomach ulcer and the number of some old slapper in Sausalito. Meanwhile in St Lucia, the accountant who administered the band's finances is enjoying fast cars, private planes, vintage champagne and loose women till he's purple in the face. Perhaps old Stocky was right all along.

On top of these worrying signs we had another problem to contend with. I'd managed to complete an academic record remarkable only for its lack of remarkability with three unremarkable A-level grades in English, geography and economics. Thanks to some feverish activity in the clearing system, I had managed to obtain a place to study English, American studies and classical civilisation at university. This was going to involve leaving home and moving into student accommodation in Manchester. Initially I'd decided to relocate to the deepest south of England, just to experience the culture shock and learn the language, but my results didn't come up to scratch and so I had to abandon plans to emigrate to Nottingham. However, I was determined to live in the halls of residence and began to look on the close proximity to Bolton as a positive advantage. Not only was it easier to take my washing home, but we could keep the band going if I travelled back on a regular basis for rehearsals. Stig and Paul weren't so sure. They thought a band should be a local posse going to the same pubs, clubs and gents' outfitters as each other and that our gang mentality would suffer if we had to be separated by long distances. This seemed unnecessarily dramatic to me, especially as I was only moving eleven miles away. Even though several members live on different continents, Def Leppard manage to keep going. I'm not suggesting that this is necessarily a good thing, but they've shown more staying power than Stig or Paul, who I began to suspect were looking for a reason to bail out. Paul, in particular, had kept his distance since that party at his house when I inadvertently lost my tea and several pints of Merrydown over his mum's slippers. Come on, we've all done it. In any case, I wasn't about to throw away the chance of three years of state-subsidised hedonism for the prospect of a Tuesday night residency at the Gardener's Arms.

4

Ridiculous and Jones

So it was that I set off to seek my fortune in the big city with a red and white spotted handkerchief knotted on a stick over my shoulder, which made carrying two suitcases extremely difficult. In principle, Zoot Suit and the Zeroids were still intact, but we were never to play together again, which must have been very distressing for our faithful followers to whom I now apologise unreservedly. Sorry, Tex. Sorry, Bong.

I moved to a hall of residence called Woolton, which had an all-male population in order that further education should not undermine the excellent grounding in being awkward in the company of women that I'd been given at grammar school. Arriving there on a blustery autumn afternoon, the accommodation did not look promising. Four rooming blocks surrounded a central building consisting of several dual-purpose facilities. There was a bar that doubled as a television lounge, a dining-hall that doubled as a throbbing discothèque on Saturday nights, and a table-tennis room that doubled as an opium den. All the buildings in the complex were constructed from bricks that resembled Keith Richard's skin in that they had a charmless pasty hue and looked as though they could give way at any moment. The roofs were fashioned from some unpleasant-looking metallic substance in a particularly offensive shade of green, which over time had become peppered with patches of comparatively attractive rust where water had run down from the ridge tiles. It looked like people had been standing up there urinating, which, it later transpired, was an eminently feasible explanation.

On arrival, I was instructed to go to the porter's lodge, which proved to be a facility doubling as a cupboard where mops and buckets were kept, but which, on closer examination, also contained a septuagenarian liver-spot collector who'd obviously been exhumed to help with the new influx. Scraping the rheum from his bloodshot eyes, he checked my name on the list before a creaking sound heralded his rising from the chair. Whether this creaking emanated from the antiquated chair or its occupant's ancient bones was difficult to tell. He began to move towards the opposite wall at a speed roughly equivalent to a slow-motion replay at a televised crown-green bowling tournament, before summoning what meagre strength was left in his wasted muscles to lift my allotted key from its hook. He also, much to my astonishment, issued me with a black gown of the type worn only by school masters in posh public schools or *Carry On* films. He informed me, in the course of a sentence punctuated by a spectacular variety of bronchial expostulations, that I would be required to wear this archaic garment each evening at dinner. By which he meant tea. Evidently the linguistic quirks of southern England applied to all universities, even those in the north. In the course of time we came to appreciate those gowns, which proved, like everything else at Woolton, to have a dual purpose.

Not only did they protect your clothes from dollops of mashed potato catapulted from other tables during tea, by which, southern readers, I mean dinner, but they could also be worn to Damned concerts in vampiric homage to lead singer Dave Vanian.

My allocated cell was on the ground floor of a low-security wing at the end of a long corridor, the floor of which was elegantly upholstered in battleship-grey lino embellished with occasional cigarette burns. The room itself contained a single bed that appeared to be struggling to bear the weight of the candlewick bedspread, a desk and chair rescued from a skip outside a refurbished hostel for the homeless, a bookcase constructed from prime balsa, a lamp that had only recently been converted from running on gas and a bemused schoolboy from Bolton feeling distinctly lonely.

Looking back on it, I think these feelings of loneliness stemmed mainly from the fact that there was no one else there. Trudging up and down the corridor to make unwanted cups of tea in the limescale-riddled kettle in the communal galley kitchen, it was a good two hours before I saw another living soul. And then it was a Christian. He was a third-year called Don Ludlow who conned his way into my room by pretending to be an average friendly chap before producing some pamphlets entitled 'Jesus Loves You' and 'Mother Mary Cares for You' and 'John the Baptist Thinks You're a Top Bloke'. He then invited me to a social get-together that evening at the chaplaincy, where there would be nibbles and fortifying beverages. At this point I had no idea what unexplored avenues of bad behaviour lay before me, but I was pretty certain the shining path of misdemeanours was not going to open unto me at the Christian Fellowship cheese and wine shindig.

It was while I was escorting this religious zealot from the premises that I ran into another human being, whom I seized upon with what must have seemed unnatural relish.

'Hi, Mark Radcliffe from Bolton. English, American studies, classical civilisation,' I blurted with outstretched sweaty palm.

'Erm, yes, hmm, Nigel Douglas from Doncaster. Geography,' responded my agitated victim. It was as if we were auditioning for *University Challenge*, but I've never been so grateful for conversation in my whole life. Throughout the remainder of the afternoon we sat in my room watching other wide-eyed innocents arrive with parents in car coats carrying scatter cushions, cheese plants and rolled-up posters of that girl in tennis gear scratching her bottom. The only exception was the rotund American Joe Devaney, who moved into the room next to mine with a stereo system that the Grateful Dead would gladly have performed open-air concerts through, and pennants brandishing the names of obscure teams like the Dallas Cowboys, the Miami Dolphins, the Cincinatti Wildebeests and the Tallahassee Arsewipes.

Nigel Douglas passed the time by browsing through my records and seemed suitably impressed with my eclectic and often deliberately obscure selection. He enthused particularly over the Stackridge section, while revealing that his personal preference was for Greenslade. It was probably at this point that the alarm bells started ringing, but for now he was the only friend I had and his musical proclivities would just have to be tolerated. While Nigel Douglas was admiring my gatefold Edgar Broughton Band sleeves, I occupied myself with admiring Nigel Douglas's bushy beard. At the age of eighteen, being able to grow a beard was just about the most virile thing a spotty undergraduate could do. Not only did it conceal whole ranges of pustulant peaks, but it had to be a sure-fire winner with female freshers, who could easily be convinced that you were a hirsute second year who'd really seen a thing or two. I myself had only managed a few wisps of gibbon's pube on my chin by this stage, and it would be well into the third year with finals fast approaching before I could attempt a respectable Zapata moustache. Nige and I never became good mates, but for that first afternoon he consoled himself in my records while I curled up for comfort in his Captain Birdseye beard.

As we went in for dinner (tea) that night, there was one room still unoccupied on our corridor. Returning two hours later and scraping the impacted peas from my gown, I noticed the lights were on in the last remaining isolation unit and decided to walk in and introduce myself in the manner that had proved so successful with Nige 'ZZ Top' Douglas. I knocked on the chipboard door and walked in proffering a ketchup-stained paw.

'Hi, Mark Radcliffe from Bolton. English, American studies, classical civilisation.'

From behind the wardrobe door came the sound of an expertly delivered fart followed by a deeply resonant belch, after which a mop of blond hair appeared and the face under it said, 'Phil Walmsley from Poulton. Building science and stuff. Fancy a tab?'

Well, this was more like it. A fellow Lancastrian who broke wind as a greeting and offered you cigarettes. Sliding a filter from the outstretched packet of ten Bensons, I quickly took in the contents of the room, not least the cloud of noxious gas that had recently escaped from my new acquaintance's anus. On the wall was a picture of the Rolling Stones, on the floor was a Dansette record player, in the open wardrobe was a particularly nasty selection of paisley Y-fronts and leaning against the bed, oh joy of joys, was an electric guitar.

'You're a guitarist, then?'

'Yeah, I can play a bit.'

'And you like the Stones, eh?'

'Best rock'n'roll band ever, mate.'

'And you still play their records on the old-fashioned gramophone?'

'They sound more authentic that way.'

'And you've got really poor taste in underpants, I see.'

Well, we were getting on, if not like a house on fire then certainly like a small dormer bungalow that was smouldering a bit. It turned out that Phil had been in a group, too, the much-vaunted cabaret combo Warlock, who'd gigged all along the Fylde coast. Like my fellow Zeroids who'd been dubious about my commitment, so Phil's erstwhile colleagues had cast him out of the coven after he was unable to make a prestigious booking at the Flagship Showbar.

Outwardly Phil and I were quite different. Despite my registration at the practice of the good Dr Feelgood, I was still something of a trainee hippy in appearance. I wore suede desert boots, brushed-denim flares and cheesecloth shirts. I was also desperately trying to grow my hair, although the top layer seemed to mutate considerably faster that the rest, lending my barnet a more than passing resemblance to a large mushroom. It was as if a hard-up Third World republic had undertaken secret nuclear testing on my head. If Inspiral Carpets had been in existence I'd have been in good company, but at that time I just looked like a dork. Phil, on the other hand, was a bit of a northern soul boy. His blond hair appeared to have been parted down the middle with a hatchet, and his tight cap-sleeved T-shirt and multi-belted Oxford bags gave way to highly polished shoes, the exceptional width of which would have ensured a safe passage across the polar ice-cap. He also had a car, which in the coming months he would park near the main gates and tinker with incessantly. He knew absolutely nothing about basic auto maintenance, but this wasn't the object of the exercise. Phil reckoned that if he hung about the gates with the bonnet open he'd catch the eye of any female students walking past. If everything went according to plan, these impoverished girls armed only with bus passes would be so impressed that he owned a car that they would offer him small sexual favours in return for a lift to the student's union. Like an angler waiting patiently for a bite, he spent many hours in his large square driving glasses, getting his hair full of sump oil, performing unnecessary adjustments with a socket spanner. That attractive, intelligent, cultured young women should pay any attention to a red-faced, bog-brush-haired grease monkey in National Health spectacles rummaging under the engine of an Austin 1100 always seemed like a bit of a long shot to me, but hell, it was worth a shot.

Phil and I started to spend a lot of time together, sharing our deep love of rock'n'roll, playing each other records that expressed something deeply personal to us in between downing pints in one and orchestrating synchronised guffs. You know, just normal matey stuff. What really began to absorb us, though, were the reports in the music press about a new breed of snotty young bands who were being swept to power on a manifesto of spitting, making a very loud noise and introducing compulsory euthanasia for Rod Stewart. We'd been absolutely entranced by a group we'd heard John Peel play on the radio called the Ramones, four teenage lobotomies from New York who played up to seventeen songs in a half-hour set. We started to hear about the Clash, the Sex Pistols and the Adverts in London, and Buzzcocks, Slaughter and the Dogs and the Fall in Manchester. What we needed was to experience some of this music first-hand, but all we seemed to get at the student's union was Renaissance, Dire Straits or Roy Harper.

Eventually, word got round that a bona fide punk band from down south was coming to play at a well-known public lavatory known as the Squat, located a stone's throw from the union, most of the stones having been thrown through the windows. The venue got its name after a group of students occupied it to save it from demolition, although once inside you'd have come to the conclusion that resistance had ultimately proved futile and the wrecking gangs had moved in. Queuing up to pay our entrance fee of thirty pence, we read for the first time, on a handwritten poster, that the band were called the Stranglers. We later found out that they'd originally been the Guildford Stranglers, formed, as they were, in Chiddington.

In contrast to the speed of service I'd been used to at BIT, the bar staff at the Squat were the very model of efficiency. They moved in a blur to create a production line of warm, watery pints of bitter in plastic glasses driven either by an extraordinary desire to serve or large amounts of amphetamine sulphate, and quite conceivably both. Having purchased two pints each, personal expenditure on the evening rapidly approaching a pound, we drank one, spilt the other and returned to the bar to buy four more before settling down in front of the stage to await the arrival of the band. We could hardly contain our excitement, for here at last in the flesh we were about to see four stick-thin snotty young oiks play ferocious music at a hundred miles an hour while flinging themselves around the stage with little or no regard for their own safety.

Sadly, we got the Stranglers. In the course of my top showbusiness career I've since met Jet Black, the drummer, and he is enormously personable as well as personally enormous. I bear him no malice at all, a sentiment I hope he'll reciprocate as he's built like a brick shithouse. However, that night in the Squat I wanted, I needed, to see a scrawny little psycho leathering the kit, not a bulbous, grumpy-looking middle-aged bloke with a grey beard. For a minute I thought it was Dave Lee Travis up there. The organist Dave Greenfield looked even worse. Never mind spring chickens, this geezer was no autumn rooster. Perched behind a battered Hammond with his Fu Manchu beard, flaccid plait and miserable countenance, he looked like a washed-up luvvie who'd just failed an audition for *Aladdin*. The two blokes up front at least had the decency to be thin, but they didn't strike us as having any great relevance to the *Zeitgeist*, which was a pretty telling observation as we had no idea what the *Zeitgeist* was, unless it was a Kraut rock band we'd yet to come across. The singer Hugh Cornwell looked like an undertaker who had a bit of a meths habit, while bass player Jean-Jacques Burnel, the youngest of the bunch by a decade or two, had a rip across the chest of an otherwise pristine black T-shirt and the sort of pudding-basin haircut barbers give small boys while their fathers are engrossed in *Amateur Photographer*'s 'How to Shoot Better Bare Breasts' section. The sense of disappointment was palpable; we'd seen bands on *The Old Grey Whistle Test* who looked younger than this. The music, too, seemed strangely sluggish, although in fairness it was difficult to tell amid the sound of plastic glasses raining on to the stage. At one point Jean-Jacques Burnel picked up one of the offending receptacles and held it aloft while proclaiming 'Yeah – plastic glasses, thrown by plastic people in a plastic world.' If we'd have been to the launderette to do our washing, we'd have had clean socks. If we'd had clean socks, we'd no doubt have gone out wearing some that night. Had we been wearing socks, we'd have laughed them off.

It's not often you can say you've paid thirty pence for a gig and considered yourself soundly robbed, but that was how we felt. It might not sound a lot now, but you have to remember that in those frugal student days thirty pence would buy you a bag of chips, a raffia shoulder purse and a copy of *Sir Gawain and the Green Knight*, which was a set text for English scholars and not a concept album by Gentle Giant.

'Well, that was a waste of time, eh, Sparky,' said Phil, who'd bestowed upon me his personal pet name, 'and we've missed *Opportunity Knocks* on the telly.'

'Dead right, Wammo,' I responded, carefully inserting his hand-crafted nickname, 'we'll never hear anything from them again.'

Towards the end of that year, a record called 'Grip' began to turn up with some regularity on the radio. It had aggression, it had a great tune and it had a keyboardist who appeared to be attempting to play every single note on the piano during the course of the song. We thought it was a corker and were absolutely astounded to hear that it was by the very same Stranglers. In a way, they were an inspiration in that we thought, 'Well, if they can do it, anyone can.' In a sense, that crystallised the punk ethic. It didn't matter how old you were, what you looked like or how well you could play. If you had something to say, you got up and said it. A bit like a Quaker meeting. At the time of writing, fully twenty years on, the Stranglers are still a going concern, albeit one that has ceased to trouble the compilers of the hit parade. You'd also have to say that they look all right, but then it's much easier to age gracefully in pop if you looked ancient to begin with.

The Stranglers débâcle served only to steel our resolve. We had to see a top-flight punk band in action to understand what it was all about, and the cavalry arrived when Johnny Thunders came to town. Johnny Thunders was lead guitarist with the New York Dolls, a glam Stones managed by Malcolm McLaren who released two electrifying albums in the early seventies. Of these, the first is particularly worth buying, not least for the photo on the back in which Johnny appears to have a cucumber and two pomegranates down the front of his Spandex trousers. Following the demise of the Dolls, Thunders had formed the Heartbreakers with his old drummer Jerry Nolan and Richard Hell, formerly of Television. By the time they reached England to play the Sex Pistols' aborted Anarchy tour of 1976, Hell had left and been replaced on bass by Billy Rath with another guitarist, Walter Lure, completing the line-up. They were booked to play in Liverpool at a club called Eric's, which would later become immortalised as the birthplace of Echo and the Bunnymen, the Teardrop Explodes and Wah! Heat, and we decided to go over and meet up with some mates of Wammo's who were travelling down from Blackpool.

Come the big night, we put on our least-flared jeans, our grubbiest T-shirts, and, using a mixture of sugar and water, coaxed our hair into a series of gravity-defying spikes which looked as though they might well have been the result of prolongued electric-shock therapy. Having spent several hours making it look like we'd just fallen out of bed, we climbed into the Austin 1100 and set off for Liverpool. As we travelled along Wilbraham Road in that little racing-green beauty, I listened to Wammo rolling on and on about what a great piece of babe bait his car was and, being a good mate, I happily concurred that the rapidly failing light was the only reason young women weren't flinging themselves across the windscreen as we passed through Stretford.

'Drive through here in broad daylight, Wammo, and you'll be beating 'em off with a stick.'

Eric's was a club with some heritage. Visionary impresario and very tall bonkers person Roger Eagle had been putting bands on there since the legendary Cavern, located directly opposite down a dimly lit back alley, had closed down. In those days Liverpool seemed the perfect setting for new musical revolution, because no self-respecting punk band would be photographed anywhere except amid a pile of rubble on a demolition site. Obligingly, Liverpool provided a pile of rubble on every street corner. Even the site of the world-famous Cavern resembled a bomb crater, and

I remember thinking that this was a particularly British phenomenon. In the States the old Cavern would have been the centre-piece of a thirty-acre theme park, but being England, bus-loads of Japanese tourists were travelling halfway across the world to photograph some heaps of bricks through a fence of chicken wire. It was all very touching somehow, although don't travel down to see the rubble now because it's all been tarted up in a big way.

Inside Eric's you could barely move, but we managed to locate Wammo's mates, whose hairstyles also owed a debt to Tate & Lyle. One of them, Ken, had such a bad complexion that it looked like he had scales, and with his hair spiked up as well I initially suspected a bizarre genetic experiment which had involved his head being replaced with a pineapple.

When the Heartbreakers hit the stage, we could only see the heads and shoulders of Johnny Thunders and Walter Lure as they bombarded backwards and forwards across the tiny stage in a series of perfectly executed jerks. If we thought our hairstyles were remotely cool, we were soon disarmed of this opinion when we saw the great god Thunders, who appeared to have a well-groomed porcupine sitting on his head. From where we were standing we couldn't see the other two members of the band, because Nolan the drummer was sitting down and Rath the bass player was a right short-arse.

As they exploded into 'Chinese Rocks', quickly followed by 'Born to Lose', it became quite clear that this was what we'd been waiting for. To be fair to the Stranglers, the Heartbreakers were knocking on a bit as well, but their energy belied their advancing years. They'd also managed to stay thin, although in the case of their leader, I imagine the heroin helped. Ultimately, Johnny Thunders became

79

another rock'n'roll casualty when he died in 'drug-related circumstances' in New Orleans in 1991. I'm not going to mythologise him, but when we next saw him playing at Rafters in Manchester he strode out on to the stage with his black leathers, cool haircut and low-slung guitar and, pausing by his amplifier only to put down the bottle of Jack Daniel's and turn every knob up to ten, he was, to us, the personification of all things rock'n'roll.

At the risk of gratuitous name-dropping, I'd like to say here that I was proud to call him a friend. Well, not a friend exactly, more a kindred spirit who I'd chat with from time to time. Well, all right then, once. It was in the toilets at Rafters when I suddenly found myself at the next urinal to the man himself, and we fell into easy conversation, as soul brothers often do. The boy looked at Johnny and said, 'What time are you on, then, Johnny?'

Johnny looked straight ahead and said, 'About eleven, I guess.'

Well, it wasn't much in the way of words, but somehow we developed an unspoken bond there which I'm sure he'd be happy to confirm if he wasn't, unfortunately, dead.

Back at Woolton Hall, Wammo and I began to lay plans to jump on the punk bandwagon. Firstly, we were going to have to undergo a radical change of image. Flared trousers just weren't acceptable any more, as Mark Sayers found to his cost when I took him to see the Jam at another legendary northern punk mecca, the Electric Circus. Untutored in the new dress code, Stocky turned up in a pristine white hooded sweatshirt, jeans containing enough material to propel two small sailing dinghies and the sort of unforgivable gleaming white clogs favoured only by dental receptionists and Brian May out of Queen. With the looks he got that night, I thought he was going to get battered before the band even appeared. As it was, he managed to avoid physical assault until the journey home on the night bus when I smacked him one. White clogs indeed.

The search for drain-pipe jeans proved initially fruitless as we trawled round every chain store in Manchester looking at endless pairs of denims which turned into wigwams below the knee. It was only while trudging the back streets to catch the bus home that we stumbled on a grubby, practically subterranean emporium known as Famous Army & Navy Stores. I can only assume that the original proprietors had been Terry and Doris Famous, because there seemed to be no other logical explanation for the name. In a basket outside they had pairs of denims that had obviously been in stock since the First World War and which they'd now stuck on the pavement in the hope of attracting those whose jobs required sturdy rather than stylish clothing. People like garage mechanics, road labourers and sociology lecturers at colleges of further education. Rummaging under the sign that tantalisingly, in its direct simplicity, stated 'Men's Jeans, £2', we hit gold. The youngish assistant, presumably Terry and Doris's eldest, Darren Famous, seemed amazed and delighted to have shifted what he'd obviously considered to be unshiftable stock. If he'd waited another six weeks, when the high-street shops filled up with straight-legs, he'd have sold them for £20 a pair. Tough luck, buster.

The shirts proved easy (Oxfam), as did the plastic toe-capped plimsolls (Woolworths). What proved less easy was facing the marauding hordes of potato-flinging, flare-wearing dingbats at dinner (tea). Wrapping our gowns tightly around us, we strode confidently into the dining-hall and walked a full yard and a half before the laughter started. You probably think I'm making this up, but you will just have to take my word for it when I tell you that wearing drain-pipe jeans that night caused as much of a rumpus as if we had been stark naked.

'Oi! Dickheads! Fancy dress ball's not till March.'

'Hey, nice strides – where'd you get them? Woolworths?'

This brought forth a prompt denial. If the accusation had been directed at the footwear, they'd have got us. Joe Devaney, being American, hurled in a series of insults that he seemed to find wholly satisfying but which no one else understood at all: 'Yo, you pinko blueberry-muffin munchers, you couldn't do a sunny-side up for the Minnesota Moose Maulers,' or something equally mystifying along similar lines.

Still, no one said being a leader of fashion was easy. People used to laugh at John Galliano. In fact, they still do, but you get the drift. To complete the transformation, Wammo and I cut each other's hair with a pair of nail scissors and a rusty Bic razor. He actually emerged reasonably intact with a tousled, tangled affair that was only lop-sided if you looked at him head-on. I came off considerably worse with a style that was somewhere between Dave Hill out of Slade and Rowan Atkinson in the first series of *Blackadder*. To this day I have no idea how Wammo managed to cut a perfectly semicircular fringe like that without following the outline of a dinner plate. Still, I eventually took it all in good humour and helped him put the wardrobe back the right way up, it having been inadvertently thrown over during the accidental tantrum that ensued in the immediate aftermath of the haircut from hell. Wammo and I have remained close friends ever since, but I've never forgiven him for that fringe. Despite the fact that these days I'd be grateful for any fringe at all.

Suitably transformed, we set about recruiting other musicians for the band. We knew that somewhere on those barren corridors like-minded souls would be lurking, ready to burst out in a yelp of teenage discontentment. Accordingly we put a notice outside the dining-hall reading: 'Wanted. Thrusting young bucks for brat punk band. Attitude essential. Uncompromising hairstyle obligatory. Musical ability optional. No fat Americans. Contact Mark or Phil.' The response to this appeal was reasonably encouraging in that three people came forward. In the absence of my drum-kit I'd decided to be the lead singer with Wammo at my shoulder with his trusty sunburst CMI Les Paul copy. What we were looking for was a bass player and a drummer with spiky hairdos and prominent cheek-bones. What we got was a chubby trombonist called Nev who later went on to play with English National Opera, a pudding-basin-haired cellist called Piers and a smoothie from Bradford named Malik who showed a keen interest in Latin American percussion. If we'd been recruiting for the new Hawkwind, we'd have been in business. As it was, we were quite clearly, for the time being at least, going to have to do it on our own, and accordingly, Ridiculous and Jones were born.

5

She Cracked

Ridiculous and Jones was an act inspired by, and infused with, the punk ethic, combining a stripped-down, energetic sound with confrontational presentation. The inclusion of inept conjuring tricks served to provide an allegorical comment on the deceptions perpetrated against the contemporary populace by governmental illusionists and to pad out a set which would otherwise have lasted about twelve minutes. Which would have been around ten minutes too long for most people.

For some weeks Phil and I had been composing songs in his room after dinner. He'd sit on the bed and strum his unamplified guitar and I'd improvise the words while scraping impacted carrot and swede purée from the back of his neck. For some reason he became a particular target for expressly couriered food parcels, which may have been a result of the night he emptied his nostrils into the soup. He didn't mean to, it was just that, laughing hysterically while suffering from a heavy cold, he inadvertently dispatched two torrents of nasal guacamole into the communal tureen. Everyone present developed an instant lack of appetite, but

Mark Radcliffe

I don't really understand what their problem was. The soup was pea and ham, so it was thick and green with bits floating in it to begin with.

So far we'd completed five songs, the titles of which will be all too familiar to proud owners who cherish their *Ridiculous and Jones Big Beat — The Burnage Wall of Bricks* bootleg cassettes. The most direct, primal punk moment was 'Breakfast in Bondage' with its opening lyrical salvo that still sounds like a rallying call to this day:

> I've got nothing to do tonight,
> I'm gonna give my granny a fright,
> I'm gonna hit her on the head with a frying pan with an
>   egg in it.

Well, it's got everything, hasn't it? From the 'nothing to do' expression of disenfranchised adolescent boredom, to the subversive 'give my granny a fright' reference to distorting the mores of polite society, right through to the solitary egg of individualism imprisoned by the iron frying pan of capitalism. When he heard lyrics displaying such clarity of thought and acute political awareness, Mr Voice-of-a-generation's-angst Joe Strummer must have been shitting himself.

In truth, our other rudimentary classics were less true to the prevailing punk philosophy. 'Nashville, Tennessee' was an ingenious barbed attack on the repetitive subject-matter of country and western music:

> Well, I went to see my auntie in Nashville, Tennessee,
> She said your uncle's here in Nashville, Tennessee,

And when I walk down the main street in Nashville,
   Tennessee,
All the signs say Nashville, Tennessee.

I've been trying to get Garth Brooks to cover it for years now.

On top of this we had the ill-advised cod-funk work-out of 'Make Love, Not Food' and two heart-stoppingly beautiful ballads in 'Lagoon Romance' and 'Alpine Woman, Mountain Bullock'. These two defining moments in twentieth-century popular music were written with the Woolton Hall audience in mind. Most of this select company were colossal rugby-playing psychopaths with no discernible necks, whose idea of a good night out was drinking seventeen pints through each other's jock-straps. The narrative thrust of these songs was therefore rich in explicit sexual detail, which good taste, making a late but welcome appearance, prevents me from repeating here. To give you a flavour, I can let you see a verse of 'Lagoon Romance', but in much the same way as competitions on the backs of cereal packets ask you to 'complete the following phrase in no more than ten words', I'll leave you to complete the last line in no more than four.

> I never thought to ask of your sweet name
> So we could meet 'neath that lonely palm again,
> The soothing sound of the lapping sea,
> You spread your buttocks and——

Well, move over, Noël Coward.

Suitably armed with such a wealth of quality material, we

87

arranged our first performance in the junior common room at Woolton Hall. Technically, our first public outing as our alter egos Billy Ridiculous and Bonneville Jones came when we shredded the red plastic innards of a road cone and visited flats occupied by girls in neighbouring Oak House attempting to sell, door to door, the small scraps of Ministry of Transport property as joke scabs. There are times when I've tried to justify this as an elaborate work of situationist performance art, but it's more easily explained as the embarrassing actions of two pillocks who couldn't hold their ale.

Our first gig proper was going to take place on a Sunday night in the bar on a stage built from trestle dining-tables. We'd managed to convince the social secretary, a pot-bellied zoologist known as Catweazle, that we should go on last, which meant that our dubious services would not be required until around ten o'clock. However, with the bar being open from five, we thought we'd nip in for a bit of a 'livener' to give ourselves some much-needed Dutch courage. By nine-thirty we'd had so many pints of Holstein livener that we were as Dutch courageous as newts, and the succession of support acts, including Piers on the cello accompanied by Malik on maracas, and numerous third-year dullards in woolly jumpers droning interminable Cat Stevens songs, slipped by in a haze. By the time we took the rickety stage, the idea of having a drink to eradicate our nerves had proved to be a masterstroke of planning as we were as incapable of feeling nerves as we were of standing up straight.

Sartorially we set trends that night which have yet to catch on, even now. I wore a crimson quilted smoking-jacket with embroidered dragons on the lapels that I'd picked up from the Cancer Research charity shop around the corner. I can only assume that one of the Wilde family had been clearing out the attic and had dropped off some of their Oscar's old clobber. With my hair suitably teased into improbable spikes with the aid of the usual sugar and water, I completed the outfit with an oversized pair of wellingtons and my striped, winceyette pyjama bottoms. Phil wasn't as cool as me. He wore a yellow chequered hunting waistcoat with a pair of cavalry twill trousers from which he'd amputated one leg. On his head he had placed an indoor television aerial, which was secured with an old school tie knotted under his chin. With this unlikely cranial appendage, his perky pink complexion and lager-distended belly, he looked like an early prototype of the Teletubbies.

Bounding on to the stage to our chosen introduction music, the theme tune to *Steptoe and Son*, we blazed into 'Breakfast in Bondage' with a ferocity that frankly surprised even us. Even more surprising, the assembled throng of fellow inmates and their girlfriends greeted the spectacle before them with generous applause and alcohol-induced guffaws. Barely pausing for breath, although managing to throw down another free pint of Holstein Export, we careered through 'Make Love, Not Food' and 'Nashville, Tennessee' with the audience reaction growing, if anything, even stronger. In truth, their unquestioning support was probably too vociferous. If there had been a few dissenting voices in the crowd, we may not have attempted the climax to the conjuring part of the show. The amazing appearing-shoe trick and the toilet roll of mystery went pretty well, as did the borrowing, from a member of the audience, of a pristine white handkerchief, which was returned to its owner only after having been magically expectorated on to. After yet more rampant cheering and rancid Holstein, Wammo turned to me and whispered, 'Let's do the disappearing male genitalia.'

The disappearing male genitalia was a masterful illusion we'd been working on for some time, and I'm amazed that David Copperfield is yet to include it in his act. This masterpiece of the prestidigitator's art consisted of removing one's trousers and underpants, showing the old block and tackle to the members of the audience and inviting them to have a good feel to check that all the props were genuine, an invitation rarely accepted. The grand wizard's nether regions were then covered with a piece of material, in this case a tea-towel displaying poor likenesses of the Brontë sisters and a view of the village of Haworth employing dubious perspective. While the shroud of intrigue was so placed the perpetrator's genitals were thrust backwards between his legs, leaving only a pubis mundus at the front elevation. Removing the loincloth with a theatrical flourish, the rapt onlookers were then invited to show their amazement at the disappearance into the ether of the offending meat and two veg. However, with a knowing wink and a wily wag of the finger, the toast of the Magic Circle then turned around and illustrated in graphic detail the actual location of the family jewels. The whole heady display then climaxed with an energetic star jump, during which all the pertinent parts were restored to their rightful place.

Well, we'd never have done it if we hadn't been carried along on a wave of euphoria and free beer, but do it we did. The reaction to this pageant was one of stunned disbelief followed by riotous applause, during which Piers the cellist ushered his fresh-faced girlfriend from the room. To be honest, we were so well oiled we didn't regret this element of our performance until the next morning. Travelling on the bus up to college, we sat opposite two willowy honeys who established immediate eye contact and emitted the occasional demure giggle.

'Blimey, we're in here,' said Phil, ever the optimist.

It wasn't until we were getting off and plucking up the courage to ask them out that they turned to us and said, 'Good gig last night, boys. Yes. Very brave to show all you've got when it's as little as that.'

Talk about feeling small. Well, that's what they were doing.

Nevertheless, on stage things were going from strength to strength and people were already beginning to compare us to John Otway and Wild Willy Barrett, and there can be few greater compliments than that. Our medley from *Grease* was a triumph as Wammo donned a floral-print skirt to play Sandy opposite my Travolta-eclipsing portrayal of Danny, for which I donned a leather jacket into the shoulders of which, for reasons I find hard to pinpoint now, a cushion had been inserted to give me the gait of a hunchback. No sooner had we sprinted through 'Greased Lightning', and removed our mate Rhys Davies and his moped from the stage, than we rounded proceedings off with the elegiac 'Lagoon Romance'. Calling for two stools from the bar, along with four more pints, we sat down to lend the end of the evening a poignant air. Unfortunately, one leg of my stool disappeared down a crack between two of the trestle tables constituting the stage and I tumbled backwards, landing what would have been heavily had the impact not been cushioned by the back of my head.

For a time our auspicious success afforded us some privileges in the corridors and cloisters of Woolton Hall. We had drinks bought for us, we had rugby full-backs who offered to roadie for us, and when Joe Devaney and a burly Cornishman called Phil Petherick collected everyone's underpants from the laundry room and put them in an oven pre-heated to gas mark seven, he left ours well alone. At least, I like to think this was a generous-hearted gesture and not just a general fear of going anywhere near Phil's paisley monstrosities for a practical joke or any other purpose. Our elevated status did not, however, avert the continued culinary bombardment, and only the following week I missed a tutorial on the metaphysical poet Andrew Marvell after being dealt a blow in the eye in a freak flying-rissole incident. To a degree we revelled in our new-found popularity, but there was a yearning to form a real band, one that would earn the respect of our peers, who would come to see us without waiting for us to get our packets out.

In the meantime we continued to go and see every band we could. We saw the Clash, the Damned, the Vibrators, 999, Eddie and the Hot Rods, X-ray Spex, Wire, Stiff Little Fingers, Penetration, Slaughter and the Dogs, Siouxsie and the Banshees, Gang of Four and Buzzcocks, as well as the American contingent led by the Ramones, Talking Heads, Blondie, Television and honorary punk icon Jonathan Richman. The bands were of varying quality, some carrying the suspicious smell of cabaret, but the collective belief and spirit of the audience was what made the atmosphere so electric. Here were gigs where the fans were not just expected to turn up and sit in silent worship at the feet of some seriously wealthy prog-rock plonker, but were actually a part of the performance itself in the clothes they wore, the dances they executed and the opinions they expounded. There was a sense of democracy to it, a feeling that this was our revolution and we all had a share in it. I have no real experience of rave culture, but I imagine its devotees in the early days were thinking along similar lines: this is ours, this is now and things will never be the same again.

During that first summer vacation from university Phil returned to Poulton-le-Fylde, where he spent the season renewing friendships with his old muckers from the now-defunct Warlock and learning to create hideous glass-blown swans in a kiosk on Blackpool's Golden Mile. For some reason, whoever designed these charmless knick-knacks had decided that each blighted creature should carry a posy of miniature glass flowers between its folded wings. Even when experienced artisans were on duty this looked mighty peculiar, but when Wammo was on the production line the unfortunate beasts looked like a rare disease had manifested itself in bulbous growths on their backs. Mystifyingly, these elephant swans sold in substantial numbers to holidaying grannies, which proves either that senile dementia was much more common than originally estimated in those days, or that pensioners at the seaside will buy any old crap after five bottles of milk stout.

I returned to Bolton, where family connections had provided me with a plum job shifting crates of empty beer bottles round a cockroach-infested warehouse from six-thirty in the morning for £29 a week. What it is to

Mark Radcliffe

have friends in high places; in this case the charge-hand at
Cambrian Soft Drinks (empties division), Graham Smedley.
Little did my fellow toilers know of my deeply privileged
introduction into their midst. I must have leap-frogged at
least two partially sighted retards to secure that position,
which just goes to show that the old boy network really
does exist.

Most of my esteemed fellow workers were hatchet-faced
harridans who could swallow lighted cigarettes, or missing
links who had tattoos everywhere bar the palms of their
hands, and only then because the tattooist couldn't get the
needle through the thick hair growing there. However, there
was one bloke who talked to me at tea break without giving
the impression that all students were a perfectly legitimate
target for mindless violence. His name was Alan, and even
though he had hair down to his waist he knew all about the
punk movement. It also turned out that he was a drummer
who'd been knocking some ideas around with a guitarist and
a bass player, but had been unable to find a singer. After
hearing of my vocal exploits with Ridiculous and Jones, he
had no hesitation in inviting me to one of their rehearsals.
Once again, fate intervened in my journey along the rocky
road to rock'n'roll anonymity.

The house Alan shared with his elderly mother was a
small terraced affair with no distinguishing features at all
save the noise coming out of it. As I turned into their street
I could hear him pummelling his kit, which must have made
him about as popular as that thoughtless jackass who lives
diagonally opposite to me and who insists on mowing his
lawn at eight-thirty on a Saturday morning. I was let into
the house by Alan's pocket-sized mum, a simple woman

in complicated knitwear, who was evidently spending the afternoon watching a Cary Grant film on television with the volume turned up to eleven. Whether she became hard of hearing before or after her son took up the drums I never discovered.

On entering the back room and witnessing the scenes within, something struck me immediately. It was the smell. If you put three blokes in a small room and force them into physical activity you will without fail find that they produce an aroma that will take the edge off the strongest appetite. Many fans fantasise about what it must be like in the dressing-room with their idols after the concert. Take it from me, it stinks. You might be tormented Thom Yorke of Radiohead, the soaring voice of pale and sensitive youth the world over, but your feet will still empty a post-gig meet-and-greet. It may seem quite a leap from Alan Hulton's back parlour to Thom Yorke's insoles, but all I'm saying is that we all sweat and, under certain circumstances, we all pong. Except for Michael Jackson, of course, who's had all his bodily secretions disconnected by a private surgeon in Beverly Hills.

As my nostrils adjusted to this pheromonal onslaught, I narrowly avoided losing my lunch on the well-worn Axminster. It was a closely fought contest and my digestive system proved a worthy opponent, but I came through on points in the final round. Having thus recovered some equilibrium in the olfactory department, I was then able to absorb the aural experience and it was apparent that Alan Hulton was a genius on the drums. It turned out that he'd spent years drumming along to Yes and Genesis records and the resultant clinical depression had to be balanced against his virtuoso command of his instrument. He could play things with one bodily appendage that I couldn't manage with five.

The guitarist I recognised as a bloke from school called Seth Mould. He was a couple of years older than me, but had balded prematurely due to a bad nerves problem. He had also grown a huge, bristling moustache due to a bad taste problem. With his large square glasses, shapeless grey slacks and weedy roll-up cigarettes, he looked like someone's decrepit grandad who'd won a Gibson SG in a competition. Like Alan, it was obvious straight away that he was a consummate musician. He knew every chord that had ever been invented and a few more which scientists were still working on in underground bunkers in New Mexico. When he dropped comments like 'Yeah, I think that's a B flat thirteenth' into the conversation I think he was trying to blind me with science, which wasn't difficult as anything beyond E, A and B was quantum physics to me.

In stark contrast to the ease with which Seth and Alan appeared to be producing wonderful sounds from the guitar and drums, the generously proportioned bass player seemed to be coming off worst in a strenuous bout of wrestling with a Burns Black Bison, producing a series of alarming farty noises in the process. This in itself didn't surprise me, because let's face it, that's what bass players do. What astonished me was the identity of this man mountain. It was Garth! What do you mean, who? Garth! An original founder member of Manchester punk heavyweights Buzzcocks. The man was practically royalty.

Over that afternoon I began to sing a few of the songs that Seth Mould had written, while throwing in a few vocal mannerisms I'd borrowed from Andy Partridge of XTC. XTC were a power-pop, jazz-punk foursome from Swindon who proved to be the common ground on which young punks like me could share a deeply meaningful relationship with old musos like Seth and Alan. Phil and I had been to see XTC at Rafters, located perversely in a basement. I never quite worked out if this was an elaborate joke on the part of the owners (they had, after all, gone to the lengths of installing false roof beams down there), or a flaw in the design concept due to the management team being monumentally stupid or completely off their faces. Perhaps they had another venue in a far-off town like Oldham located in a light, airy loft space at the top of a refurbished warehouse complex called the Cellar or the Dungeon or the Crypt.

Anyway, one night Phil and I had descended the staircase to the attic to watch XTC do their stuff, and some stuff it was. Terry Chambers and Colin Moulding were rock solid as a rhythm section, over which Andy Partridge and Barry Andrews strangled all manner of alarming sounds from throat, guitar and keyboards. Andrews, balding and besuited, attacked a wheezing old organ that looked like it might be running off Camping Gaz. It was on a small collapsible frame and could have been an optional extra on a particularly lavish caravan.

I have no idea why, but the devices available on the modern caravan never cease to fascinate me. If you're ever on a camping holiday, which, to be honest, is a situation no sane person should ever find themselves in, a good way of passing one of your endless, drizzly days with much hilarity is to casually stroll up to a dumpy caravanner with chin-strap beard and bumbag and say, 'Nice caravan.' This, of course, like *The Les Dennis Laughter Show*, is a contradiction in terms, but it will swiftly gain the confidence of your chosen victim, especially when followed immediately by the leading question, 'And I bet it's got all the mod cons, hasn't it?' Like inviting a Jehovah's witness into a house, this will be a signal for him to show you everything he's got and explain it at great length.

'Yes, this is the combined butane-powered rotisserie and curling tongs set, which is very handy for cooking a lovely chicken before the wife does her hair if we're off to play bingo in the clubhouse.'

'Very interesting, and what's that little wonder?'

'Well, that's the portable, stowaway, fibreglass-resin, battery-operated mini-television and strip-light vanity unit, which is very handy for the wife to do her make-up while watching *Emmerdale* if we're off to a beetle drive in the clubhouse.'

'Amazing, and pray tell, my fascinating new acquaintance, what is this device in the broom cupboard here?'

'Ah, now that's the fully plunge-operational, pastel-shaded Tupperware chemical bidet, which is very handy for—'

'Don't tell me . . . the wife to wash her bottom in after she's been to the lavatory if you're off to bore people rigid in the clubhouse. Well, lovely talking to you, but now I really must go back and dig a cesspit before retiring to my damp nylon sleeping-bag cocoon to read a guide-rope catalogue by a flickering gas lamp with the radiance of your average glow-worm. Happy holidays.'

So much for Barry Andrews' organ. On guitar and vocals, Andy Partridge was a man possessed. He obviously knew as many chords as Seth Mould, but he played them with real ferocity and I remember remarking that it was amazing that he didn't break more strings:

'Those strings must be made of steel, eh, Wammo?'

'Guitar strings *are* made of steel, Mark.'

'There you are, then.'

What impressed me most of all about Partridge, though, was his voice and his trousers. He performed vocal gymnastics the like of which I've never heard; swooping, screeching, growling and generally ripping and stripping the song until it was practically unrecognisable. Their memorable rendition of 'All Along the Watchtower' would accordingly open with 'The-e-e-eee-ouuuu-there mu-u-u-st beeeeee – grrrrr – some wowowowahway out of hiya-hiya-howee-hubba-hubba-here' or guttural approximations to that effect. Equally impressive were his strides, which were white with lines of black arrows pointing up the legs showing the general 'this way to the grotto' direction to his groin. What a man.

If Alan Hulton's back room, with its polystyrene ceiling tiles and collection of wall-mounted commemorative thimbles (who commemorates something with a thimble?), lacked some of the atmosphere of the subterranean skylight club Rafters, then it certainly didn't show in the way I set about the wholesale bastardisation of Seth Mould's lyrics. One song was called 'Linda Cartwright', the chorus of which constituted a four times repetition of the line 'Linda Cartwright – she can't even play the part right'. After I'd Partridged it, the result was more like 'L-L-L-Linduuuuh C-C-C-C-Cartwrooooooowt – she ca – she ca – she cacacacacow can't even p-p-p-p-play the part-t-t-t rieeeeeeeeeeeght'.

Mystifyingly, Alan, Seth and even the right honourable

Garth decided that this was the missing piece to their musical jigsaw, and with judgement like that it's no surprise that they never quite cracked the global market. To celebrate our blissful union we adjourned to the pub for last orders, where our thickset bassist ordered two pints of Guinness and two double whiskies. 'That's nice,' I thought, or, as it was just after rehearsals, 'Th-th-th-a-a-a-t-t-ssss nnnnnnnnn-niccccce, he might be the famous one, but he'll still get a round in.' Alas, it transpired that this was his usual last order for personal consumption only. The rest of us got halves of dark mild and we retired to a leatherette banquette to discuss tactics, at which point Seth dropped not only his bumper bag of pork scratchings but also his bombshell.

'Look, lads, it's all sounding great, but it's only fair to tell you that my nerves won't allow me to play on stage. I can still be in the band and write the songs, but you'll have to find someone else to do it live.'

There was a stunned silence before we recovered our poise and offered sensitive support, encouragement and understanding:

'Well, perhaps if you sat down at the back it would be OK.'

'Maybe you could sit off-stage behind the PA.'

'Come on, you big bald woofter, just get your prick out of the custard and get on with it.'

Despite these words of comfort, he was adamant he wouldn't play in front of an audience. Unless we were planning to make a habit of performing to empty halls, and God knows we would come pretty close, this meant we had a vacancy to fill.

'Do you know any guitarists, Mark?'

*   *   *

Bearing in mind that all the songs Wammo had played up to this point consisted of either E, A and B, or C, F and G, the way he reacted to Seth's casual requests for 'F sharp major sevenths', 'E flat suspended fourths' and, on one notable occasion, 'a B flat seventh augmented ninth' showed real spunk. 'Never mind all that bollocks,' he'd ejaculate, 'just show me where to put my fingers.' Calling ourselves She Cracked after the pulsating Jonathan Richman tune, we quickly knocked together a set of angular originals which combined the prevailing attack of the new wave with every chord in the book. When our mates came to see us for the first time at the Oak House Student Flats bar, they were stunned: 'Christ almighty,' enthused Rhys Davies, 'you really aren't that shit, are you?' Woolton's noted Rasputin look-alike Nige Douglas was no less effusive when he said, 'For a bunch of dickheads it was OK, that.' Even Joe Devaney was moved to say, 'Jeez, dudes, that bitched my ass,' or something similar, which we gladly accepted as a compliment.

Basking in these and other eulogies, we really felt like we were on our way. Here at last was a band to be proud of with real presence, genuine energy, cracking songs, a bona fide punk celebrity and a drummer who was a true world-beater when he wasn't drunk or suffering an asthma attack. The occupant of the drum stool's ability might not seem that important to you, but, believe me, there's never been a truly great band that didn't have a great drummer. The only exception to this is the Beatles, as it's fair to say that Ringo Starr wasn't the best drummer in the world. It's equally fair to say he wasn't the best drummer in the Beatles. Alan Hulton, by way of

101

contrast, was a prince among percussionists, and all we would have to do as we toured the world's ice-hockey stadia was keep an inhaler handy and the cans of Kestrel locked in the fridge until after the show, and we'd be the only serious competition that Joy Division would lose sleep over.

Tragically, if predictably, it didn't work out that way. Looking back now, I can't believe how naïve we were. We genuinely thought that desperate A & R men would accost us backstage at the Russell Club, where we'd shared the bill with Biting Tongues, and beg us to sign world-wide for ten albums. We really did believe that when we sent tapes to record companies and radio stations, people would listen to them and recognise the true value of what we were doing. We thought that a two-line review in the student newspaper that read, 'She Cracked at the Solem Bar were on decent enough form before their drummer had to go outside to catch his breath,' would make the national music press sit up and take notice.

Gradually, as with most bands, the realisation that you're not going to set the world alight dawned, and rehearsals became less frequent and more torpid. The end came in the glamorous surroundings of Tyldesley Labour and Bowling Club, where Garth's mum and dad were employed as bar stewards. One night we all went down there, primarily because the beer was cheap. After ten pints or so, we were suddenly overcome by the irresistible urge to take to the stage, so Garth accosted the resident drummer Vern and asked him if we could borrow the equipment, and when I say asked, I mean he said, 'Piss off, Vern, we're on now.'

Under our encouragement, Garth agreed to sing his Tom

Jones medley, and with Ian on drums, Wammo on guitar and, inadvisably, me on bass, he bounded on stage with a silk shirt knotted across his bouncy-castle belly to launch into 'What's New, Pussycat?', while wiggling his crotch at the beehived matriarchs who were waiting for the raffle to be drawn. It was not received with the greatest of enthusiasm.

It had all gone wrong. We'd hooked up with Al, Seth and Garth as anarcho-punk, or, if you prefer, talentless cabaret artists, in the hope that their musicianship and fame would change our lives. Within a few short months it had worked the other way round. The raw promise of She Cracked had given way to the cartoon capers of Ridiculous and Jones. Once Seth and Alan recognised that, they dropped us like a stone, and I can't say that I blame them. If it hadn't been for the fact that we were us, we'd have dropped us, too.

6

Skrewdriver

In the summer following the collapse of She Cracked, I continued to live in the flat on Booth Avenue I'd been sharing with Wammo and a town-planning student from Southampton called Gerry Kitchen. Initially, Phil and I shared one bedroom, which worked out fine most of the time, but, as my cohabitee observed, would be 'pretty awkward if we got a couple of chicks back here'. Thankfully, the situation never arose. Had he managed to lure some impressionable fresh-faced theologist back to his crusty nylon-sheeted lair, I'd have been faced with the options of vacating my bed or lying awake catching glimpses of his spotty white posterior waxing and waning in the milky moonlight, and a night on the streets was preferable to that.

Before we'd moved in, we had made a point of asking the landlord if the flat was damp, to which he replied firmly in the negative. In the literal sense he was right, as 'damp' was no way to describe the prevailing conditions in that bedroom. A better description would be soaking wet. Thankfully, there was a two-bar electric fire in the hearth which featured an undulating sheet of heat-resistant plastic inexpertly daubed with black paint to resemble no fossil fuel yet successfully mined, but which was nevertheless proudly listed in the inventory as 'coal effect'. Phil's fetid futon was located much nearer than mine to this pathetically inadequate heat source, so if he braved the elements and retired to bed first, he used the room's solitary plug socket to fire it up and, over the course of an hour or so, bring the temperature of his bed to above freezing point. The sheets were still damp, of course, but at least your flesh didn't stick to the pillow as you slid in. If I plucked up the courage to put on my mittens and enter our bedroom first, and, believe you me, Sir Ranulph Fiennes would have blanched at it, then I commandeered the socket to operate my electric blanket. When selecting somewhere to lay your weary head, places where running water and mains electricity meet are probably best avoided, and there's every possibility that my bed was a potential death-trap. However, being fried alive seemed a risk worth taking just for the sheer enjoyment of watching Wammo brace himself for the shock to the nervous system that contact with his unheated sheets would inevitably bring. In retrospect, it seems extraordinary that two blokes enjoying the benefit of a university education could spend a year sharing a single-plug socket without either considering investing in a double adaptor.

Gerry, despite paying only an equal third of the £12 weekly rent, had a room of his own. This was partly due to the fact that he needed more space for his technical-drawing equipment and also because he didn't share our enthusiasm for jumping up in the morning and farting in each other's face. The most notable things about Gerry were his centre parting, evidently the result of laser surgery such was its depth and accuracy, and his blind devotion to Southampton

Football Club. He wasn't gay, he had a girlfriend called Karen Crotty, but if Mick Shannon had tantalisingly lowered his Y-fronts in the privacy of that moist brown-carpeted cell, I think he'd have discovered reserves of latent homosexuality he'd little suspected of being there. Despite being a genial and long-suffering sort of bloke, Gerry moved out relatively quickly, which put the rent up to a crippling six quid a week each. Admittedly, I gleefully contributed to his domestic discomfort, but I still maintain that it was not me who pushed him over the edge. I never tried to deny that it was me who nailed Karen's knickers to the ceiling or left a portion of macaroni cheese in his Southampton bobble hat. I hold my hands up and accept that Wammo and I were accomplices in the great emulsion paint scandal. This involved a pool of eggshell white being silently laid at the door of Gerry's room, after which a mock fight took place at high volume in the hallway. Understandably keen to see their flatmates suffer a violent beating, the young lovers scampered out to investigate, and in their speed and eagerness left a trail of ghostly footprints on the Wilton shagged pile. These things I concede, but I ask you, who was it who parted his bare buttocks and broke wind over Gerry's chicken and mushroom pie and chips during *Match of the Day*? Well, I'm not mentioning any names, but his initials are Phil Walmsley.

When Phil went home for the summer to continue his active role in the shameful conspiracy to defraud old people of their pensions in return for deformed glass-blown novelties, I opted to stay on to experiment in a little fledgling cohabitation with a blonde biochemistry drop-out from Bingley. I was also loath to leave the elaborate fungus formations we'd nurtured by meticulous daily irrigation of the kitchen wall. Settling in for a splendid summer of snogging, signing on and cider, I had the next few months mapped out until the day the telegram arrived. Hammering on the peeling door at the crack of noon, the postman thrust the envelope marked 'Urgent' into my hand before stomping off, muttering 'Bloody students' very nearly under his stagnant pond-water breath. Tearing it open, I read the stark message within: 'Phone Phil urgently. That means now, dickhead.'

'Jesus Christ,' I blurted, 'what the hell's happened? Perhaps one of his relatives has died, or maybe he's inadvertently sucked instead of blown and has got a molten mutant swan in his lungs.'

Stabbing ten pence into the slot, I could feel my voice quivering as I spoke:

'Oh, h-h-hello, M-Mrs Walmsley, I – is your Wammo there?'

'Hello, Mark. Are you all right? Are you shivering? It's not natural to be cold in July. Especially now you've got sole use of the plug socket. Now hold on and I'll get Philip for you.'

'Well, she doesn't sound like there's been a family bereavement,' I thought as I waited for Phil to come to the phone. 'Bloody hell, sodding pips are going and I'll have to put another ten pence in now. That's the price of a pint of mild I've wasted already. He'd better not be having a dump or I'll have stuck a week's dole down the bleeding thing before he's said a word.'

There was an agitated clatter at the other end.

'Sparky, is that you?'

'Of course it's me, you pillock – what's wrong?'

'Listen, I've been playing in this punk band with my old mates from Warlock and we've got a gig, but the drummer's a wanker. Will you do it?'

'Yeah, 'course I will, but why the telegram? When is this gig?'

'Saturday.'

'What day is it today?'

'Wednesday.'

'Christ almighty. Right, I'll get the train in the morning and ring you from the station. Oh, by the way, where is this gig, then?'

'It's at a festival in Groningen, which is in the north of Holland.'

'Right, well, I'll get up early, around elevenish, and I'll phone you . . . Hang on a minute, did you say Holland? Run that by me again.'

'It's a punk festival and it's in . . . beep beep beep . . . tomorrow . . . brrrrrrr.' With that the line went dead, and I certainly wasn't going to waste the price of a portion of chips phoning him back, but did he say Holland? On Saturday? Surely not.

The journey to Phil's in Poulton was as uneventful as taking a full drum-kit on a train packed with grumpy pensioners heading for Blackpool can be. The occasional obstreperous octogenarian evidently considered it inappropriate that a floor tom-tom should occupy a window-seat while elderly gentlemen with walking-sticks had to stand as far as Preston, but what could I do? I'd gallantly given up my own seat to a heavily pregnant fat lass from Widnes, and there was simply nowhere else I could put the drums, although one old-timer did have a suggestion that I informed him would prove difficult without a catering pack of Stork margarine and a good deal of discomfort. It was, then, with some joy and relief that I arrived at Poulton-le-Fylde, and there can't be many people who've said that.

Phil was waiting on the platform in a state of great agitation, sporting a pair of flared hipsters requiring immediate alteration. Hurrying me into the idling Austin 1100, he filled me in on the battle plan: 'Yeah, so me and Des and Les have got this gig in Holland through a dodgy agent from Fleetwood, but the last time we went out with the drummer Chinny he fell asleep on a toilet floor after a particularly exhausting bout of diarrhoea, and we can't bear the thought of four days in a van with an incontinent psychopathic skinhead.' Well, you could see his point.

He drove me to the tiny council house that Les Bartlett shared with his gran. In all the time I knew Les, I only ever saw him in the clothes he wore that day: a black leather waistcoat, half-mast Levis and a pair of size-twelve combat boots liberally splattered in the plaster that indicated he wasn't first and foremost a guitarist. He was a friendly sort of bloke with an ever-present grin, which could, however, appear moderately threatening if he'd forgotten to put his false front teeth in. Les's bedroom contained, quite reasonably, a bed, along with two Marshall cabinets, a sunburst Les Paul, his collection of unwashed milk bottles bearing the stamps of various assorted dairies, the cannabis plants his gran lovingly watered daily safe in the knowledge that her grandson was cultivating a forest of miniature conker trees, and Des Richards. Des had a rasping voice that was as pleasant to listen to as fingernails being scraped down a blackboard, so naturally he was the singer. He was wearing red drain-pipes, a Grenadier Guards jacket, the hairstyle of a startled spiny ant-eater and the snarling expression of an assistant behind a post office counter.

At this point I had better come clean and admit that in later life Des became a prime mover in the National Front, and with a completely different line-up played many fascist rallies under the same group name. During the weeks I spent in his company, he was actually charm personified and never once expressed any bigoted views whatsoever. Don't misunderstand me, I'm not defending the odious extremism he later adopted, it's just that there was no sign of it at this point. The name Skrewdriver is now synonymous with ultra-right-wing supremacist dogma, and that's a sad betrayal of the ideals and efforts of everyone else involved with the band in those early days. You'll just have to trust that if I (or Phil or Les) had had any inkling of the racist philosophies that came to dominate Des's thinking, then we'd have been off like a shot.

Des informed us that he'd been trying to book a local church hall for us to rehearse in, and while he'd been able to make a reservation for Friday, that Thursday evening was out because of the over-fifties badminton session. Did this sort of thing stand in the way of the Clash I wondered. It was also at this meeting that I was informed that my battle-scarred Olympic kit was surplus to requirements, as I would be using Chinny's much-admired Slingerland.

'Well, why the bleeding hell didn't you tell me that before I humped it on to the train, incurring the wrath of several psychotic coffin dodgers, who beat me savagely round the head with colostomy bags?' I enquired calmly.

Phil went red, which, in truth, for a man of his pigmentation was hardly a transformation of chameleonic proportions. 'Hmmm . . . aaah . . . yes . . . well . . . y'see . . . sorry, our kid.'

'And anyway, I thought this Chinny was a grade A nutter. How come he's lent you his prized Slingerland kit when he's not even in the band any more?'

'Hmmm . . . aaah . . . yes . . . well . . . y'see . . . we haven't actually told him he's not in the band any more.'

'Oh, I get it. You don't tell him about the gig, you just use his drums, which he's left in the rehearsal room, and steal them away to Holland.'

'Hmmm . . . aaah . . . yes . . . well . . . y'see . . . his drums aren't exactly in the rehearsal room as such.'

'So where are they, then?'

'In the shed.'

'Which shed?'

'The one behind his house.'

'So how are we going to get them, then?'

'Hmmm . . . aaah . . . yes . . . well . . . y'see . . . if Des keeps him talking at the front door, then you and me and Les can nip into the shed and chuck the drums over the back fence.'

'Right. Isn't there just one small flaw in this otherwise cunning plan?'

'What's that, then?'

'Chinny, from the little I know of him, is a pea-brained sadistic giant who, if he hears his beloved Slingerland being hurled over the garden wall, will rush round and beat the living daylights out of us.'

'Hmmm . . . aaah . . . yes . . . well . . .'

As it happened, the dreaded Chinny was out when we went round. His bespectacled, white-haired father said he'd gone to night school, which seemed extraordinarily unlikely unless the local technical college had introduced a course in adult toilet-training. Removing the Slingerland proved relatively straightforward under the circumstances, and all that remained was to learn all the songs and nip into Blackpool for Phil to buy a bass guitar, which, despite the fact that he was playing bass in the band, it had thus far slipped his mind to do. Still, it was only Thursday evening, and we wouldn't need to leave for Holland until two o'clock the following afternoon. No sweat.

Rehearsals for our début European jaunt went favourably. Les Bartlett made more noise than any guitarist I'd ever heard, obliterating the vocals entirely, which, as any member of our eventual audience would confirm, was a blessing and no mistake. Phil, despite learning the bass lines as he went along, managed to nod, shrug his shoulders and thrust his headstock in a kind of idiot semaphore to communicate the basic structure of the tunes to the rookie drummer. We ran once through the entire set, which must have consisted of ten songs or so with an average running time of one minute and fifty seconds each. On to some of these we tagged a cacophonous crescendo ending à la Lynyrd Skynyrd, which nudged them over two minutes. This meant that our total performance time was running somewhere around twenty minutes, although this didn't allow for Des's witty and inspired banter, which on a good night, so Phil told me, could add a further ninety seconds. Having absorbed the rudiments of the material, and, to be honest, the rudiments were often all there was, we went back to the first song to polish the finer points, such as starting and finishing together. I have no idea what the song was called, because at no point during rehearsal or gig did I hear one word of the lyrics. I simply listened to Les's guitar roar and took each twitch of Phil's razored blond bonce as a cue to stop or start. It sounded great from where I was. After a couple more run-throughs, that first number was sounding fairly plausible, and if we systematically worked through the remainder of the set we'd be in grave danger of appearing competent. Unfortunately, we never got the chance as at that moment the van arrived to take us to the ferry port at Sheerness. Ah well, at least we had one tune we knew people would like, which may not sound a lot, but it's one more than the Spin Doctors.

The ferry crossing was spent drinking Southern Comfort in the bar, apart from a brief excursion to the cafeteria, where sausage, beans and chips accounted for the equivalent of a week's rent. However, it was money well spent as Wammo had strongly advised lining the stomach before an extended bout of seaborne drinking, advice I greatly appreciated when losing the residue of that grease-ridden platter over the side forty minutes later. 'Jesus Christ,' I remarked, returning to the Salty Seadog Saloon wiping overpriced slurry from my lips, 'that cost me about a quid a heave.'

Our host for this intrepid expedition was an agent by the name of Jimmy Quimby. He had blond hair cut into that peculiar pudding-basin hairstyle favoured by middle-aged businessmen and football club chairmen called Francis Lee. His candy-pink Bri-nylon leisure shirt, undersized and overpressed grey slacks, and white wet-look loafers made him look as thoroughly disreputable as someone wearing sandwich boards reading 'I am thoroughly disreputable'. He talked twenty to the dozen, or perhaps even twenty-four, and snatching a few minutes of delirious sleep in the bar that night proved impossible, as no sooner had you slumped open-mouthed and spittle-chinned on a velour couchette than you would be woken with a start by the clatter of Jimmy Quimby dropping another name:

'Yes, well, of course, when I did this trip with the Stones you couldn't move for chicks . . . Groningen, yes, I remember it from the early seventies when I came with Elton . . . of course, my wife's a great singer and I've just done a deal with Clapton to play on her next record.'

Well, I knew Clapton had had some years detached from reality in a drug-addled stupor, but it seemed unlikely things had got as bad as that.

It was left to the grim-faced Des to forcefully pose the question that had been bothering all of us: 'Yes, it's very interesting, all this showbiz tackle, Jimmy, but if you're constantly dealing with Elton, Rod, Mick and Keef, then what are you doing on a rust-bucket ferry with a bunch of well-oiled wazzocks from Poulton-le-Fylde?'

Quimby smiled enigmatically and said, 'An investment in the future.' This was quite patently bullshit, as the only investment Jimmy Quimby ever made was in a bank account on the Isle of Man.

Nevertheless, years in the business had given him a certain financial acumen, which was not without its uses on tour. His ability to feed himself, two roadies and a full band for under a fiver was little short of miraculous. The trick hinged on the exploitation of a design fault found in many Dutch service stations. On collecting a tray, you immediately find yourself disappearing behind a partition to select your hot

115

food, subsequently re-emerging twenty feet further on at the drinks dispenser, before moving finally to the check-out. This gives you a good two or three minutes out of sight of the eagle-eyed assistant at the till. The plan therefore, beautiful in its simplicity, was to order fish, chips and, naturally, it being continental Europe, mayonnaise, which you would then eat in approximately ninety seconds before binning the plate in the salad bar and emerging at the pay station with a tray bearing only a small beaker of Fanta. A surreptitious cough from orchestrator-in-chief Quimby would inform you that an incriminating smudge of salad cream on the upper lip was in danger of threatening the heist. This would be rectified with a hurried wipe of the sleeve or a spectacular sneeze into a serviette, in the hope of giving the impression that you were suffering from a particularly heavy cold.

'Thanks for dinner, Jimmy,' said Wammo, wiping the mustard from his cheeks. 'Tell me, did you look after Hendrix as well as you're looking after us?'

Quimby was not amused. 'Look, son, if you're not happy, you can piss off back to England right now. I've got plenty of top acts I could be seeing to, you know.'

'I know, I'm sorry,' Phil mumbled, 'and how are the Krankies?'

By the time we reached Groningen we were ready for bed, especially Wammo, who'd completed the journey crushed between two Marshall cabinets in the back of the equipment truck. He said this was because he wanted to travel with the crew and really experience life on the road, although it may also have had something to do with Jimmy Quimby's insistence that no little smart-arse was going to travel in his Cortina Ghia.

Astonishingly, the hotel was an enchantingly bijou family-run pensione on a picturesque cobbled square. We would later learn that we owed this unexpected luxury to the promoter of the festival, who had made the bookings himself, but that didn't stop the slime-ball Quimby from standing in the lobby, palms outstretched, proclaiming, 'See, boys, don't I look after you? Now, who fancies a drink? There's a little bar round the corner where I recall me and Herman's Hermits . . .' The rest of this spurious anecdote was lost as Wammo and I bolted for the stairs in search of the twin room that would be our haven from Fleetwood's answer to Lew Grade.

The room was simply furnished with a small sash window commanding a charming vista of the tree-lined piazza without. Two single beds were made up with those starched white cotton sheets you only ever get in nice guest-houses and private hospitals, and they never felt as good as they did that night. It was while lying there contemplating our uncharacteristic good fortune that I noticed the smell. It was as if a bulimic rat had gorged itself on rancid Gorgonzola before vomiting behind the radiator. Eventually I traced the origin of this most obnoxious aroma and was able to say with some certainty that the source was Phil's baseball boots.

'Blimey charlie, Wammo, your feet reek – get those boots off and give them a good seeing to with the deodorant or something.'

'I haven't brought a deodorant,' countered Phil indignantly, 'you can't pack everything, you know.'

'Well, I'm not sleeping in the same room as those stinking boots.'

To be fair, my feet were no less fragrant than his. We'd

117

both left England in the clothes we stood up in, which meant that for the duration of our world tour our feet would be encased in matching pairs of rubber-soled Adidas baseball boots. At the time, these were considered the height of footwear fashion, but they didn't half create a pong.

'I know. It's a warm night. Let's stick our boots on the window-sill to air off till morning.'

'Nice one, Phil. I knew you'd think of something.'

As the offending boots went into meltdown on the window-ledge, sending clouds of toxic fumes into the balmy night air, I settled back into my freshly laundered linen and dreamt of the triumphant gig that would come the next day. 'Hello, Holland. Let's make some noise.'

Expecting to be awoken next morning by shafts of radiant sunlight and the gentle twittering of birds, it was a bit of a shock to be jolted out of our slumbers by the hammering rain. As any festival-goer knows, this is not exactly the best possible news on the morning of an open-air gig. Immediately, my heart went out to the poor unfortunates camped out at the festival site, who had a much grimmer day in store than they could possibly have known. The weather was an unfortunate act of God which just had to be borne with as much good humour as possible, but it was adding insult to injury making them stand there and listen to us.

'Hey, Phil, are you awake?'

He replied in the affirmative with a whipcrack of flatulence.

'It's pouring down. It's going to be a mud-bath out there.'

The ever-charitable Wammo snuggled further down into

his once pristine sheets and mumbled, 'Ah well, at least we're warm and dry.'

There followed a blissful few minutes in which we luxuriated in our good fortune before an agonised shriek from the bed to my right shattered the drizzly calm.

'Bloody hell, Sparky, the boots!'

Charging to the window and throwing up the sash, our worst fears were confirmed. Perhaps in an act of retribution for our systematic defrauding of the motorway catering establishments, the Dutch deity of the downpour had evidently waited for the onset of our slumbers before aiming the celestial hose-pipe at our footwear. They were absolutely drenched, especially Phil's right boot, which had inadvertently been placed under a crack in the guttering and was acting as a receptacle for the diluted green slime that dripped steadily through.

Descending the stairs to breakfast, we filled the hotel with a variety of loud squelching noises as if, in a double dose of Kafkaesque metamorphosis, two giant bullfrogs were making their way to the muesli. There is something particularly depressing about having wet feet, but at least we knew we could look forward to returning home in only two or three days' time to the familiar warmth of our tartan Dunlop slippers, which in Phil's case smelt even worse than the baseball boots.

Curiously, although we were starving and could savour the rare experience of dining on food which had actually been paid for, Phil and I were reticent about entering the refectory. It was full of pinched-faced pensioners who were on coach tours to places which had very little going for them. I mean, rather like, say, Huddersfield, there's absolutely nothing wrong with Groningen, but you wouldn't go there for your holidays. Maybe this was the point. If the vast majority in the party were in the process of losing their mental faculties, their ability to absorb information would be vastly reduced, so perhaps a considerate tour operator had drawn up an itinerary taking in places of no interest whatsoever. Pathetic as it sounds, Phil and I just looked at each other blankly, trying to summon up the confidence to paddle over to the cold meats and crispbreads. Why we experienced this fear, I really couldn't say. In retrospect, I'm reminded of being a child trying to overcome arachnophobia by catching a household spider, when your mum would say, 'Don't be a wimp. That little spider is much more frightened of you than you are of it,' and those little old people must indeed have been nervous about the presence of two hedgehog-headed hucksters standing in a suspicious-looking pool in the lobby.

Thankfully, help was at hand. A loud clomping sound came to our attention, followed by the sight of a large, plaster-peppered, reinforced-steel toecap appearing inside the doorway, followed some seconds later by Les Bartlett with a gob full of Emmental.

'All right, lads, come and get stuck in, there's a top trough on here. I'm on me thirds already.'

Shamefaced, we trudged damply in, leaving our slug trails behind us, and meekly made for the fruit compote. Amazing, really, that at the time the European press was carrying story after story about the hooligan hordes of punk rockers who were fearless in their thirst for confrontation, and here were we needing safety in numbers to get a hard-boiled egg from the breakfast buffet.

*   *   *

The festival site was in a tree-lined park just outside the town, and by the time we arrived the rains had abated, making me even more convinced that it had all been the act of sadistic spirits determined to douse our boots. Looking through the festival programme, the mild alarm we experienced at discovering we were the headline act turned to blind terror when we looked at the band who had topped the bill on the previous day.

'Jesus Christ, Generation X!'

Generation X was the band fronted by Billy Idol, general pretty punk pin-up and darling of the music press. We had certain things in common with Generation X: we were British, there were four of us and we were committed to the punk cause. Where we differed was that they could play pretty well. Quite how Jimmy Quimby had managed to secure us a booking as a headline act I never discovered, but I imagine lying through his teeth had something to do with it: 'Oh yes, Skrewdriver are massive in England, much bigger than the Pistols, who'll never get anywhere, bunch of little pillocks.'

The realisation dawned that we were out of our depth, which wasn't difficult, as we'd have been out of our depth in a bird-bath. To make matters worse, something he was supremely adept at, Jimmy had made sure all the publicity described us as 'the most blistering live band in Britain'. A literal European translation could have taken this to mean that seeing us perform resulted in an out-break of pustulous skin complaints, and that was a lot more likely than us being able to live up to expectations musically.

As we retired to our backstage caravan, we took the

only course of action open to bands in these circumstances, that of drinking all the free lager available in the shortest possible time. Systematically working through the Tuborg mountain, our spirits began to lift. Obviously the beer had a lot to do with it, but closer inspection of the other groups booked to appear that day confirmed that punk rock had yet to permeate this far-flung outpost. The home-grown acts appeared to be either ageing blues combos or the type of third-rate progressive nonsense we hadn't had the misfortune to experience since the heady days of BIT.

Des read the poster aloud, his voice a rising pitch of indignation: 'Leviathan. Smokey Sam's Blues Band. Apocalyptic Intervention. Big Bill's Blues Band. Smegma. Commander Olaf's Cat-Flap. Freddy and the Fire Balls. Skrewdriver – the most blistering live band in Britain!' He put the poster down and bared his teeth in a gnarled, beer-froth-infested grin. 'All this lot'll be a crock of shit. We'll just go on and play faster and louder than anyone else and we'll pull it off.'

Apart from the fact that we had no control of the overall volume, and if we played any quicker we'd be on and off inside fifteen minutes, this was just the rallying cry we needed, and for a time it seemed like his prophecy would turn out to be well judged. The succession of local bands, frozen somewhere in the late sixties, were indeed as he had so poignantly predicted, 'a crock of shit', and accordingly our new-found confidence increased in equal measure with our state of inebriation. We began to feel good, to feel cocky, to feel sure that we could show these idiots what rock'n'roll was all about. Then Freddy and the Fire Balls went on.

Freddy and the Fire Balls were a bunch of stick-thin

rockabillies from Tyne and Wear. Evidently they, like us, were innocents abroad in the clutches of an agent who was about as trustworthy as the child-catcher in *Chitty Chitty Bang Bang*, but nowhere near as handsome. Their particular sleazeball Svengali had failed to secure the necessary documentation before leaving England, which had resulted in the band's gear being impounded on arrival in the Low Countries. Prolonged and fruitless negotiations for the return of the equipment had made them hideously late, and they arrived backstage looking snotty, bereft and bedraggled, although for all we knew they looked like this all the time, and in need of a good cuddle off their mums. After disappearing with the promoter into the beer tent, they emerged several minutes later and tapped gingerly on the door of our luxuriously appointed and Oranjeboom-anointed Winnebago. Opening the door, I was confronted with these four bequiffed urchins shuffling nervously, squeezing their testicles and sucking snot up their noses. One of them opened his mouth to speak and I fully expected him to say, 'Hello, Mr Radcliffe, is your Wammo playing out?' However, what he actually said was, 'All right mate, I'm Freddy and we need to ask you a favour.'

'Yeah, all our stuff's stuck at customs 'cos of this dickhead agent,' piped Fire.

'So we were wondering if we could use your rig,' added Ball with more than a hint of desperation.

The bass player didn't say anything, but then, they never do.

Under the circumstances, we didn't have much choice. We knew how it felt to have fallen in with the Bill Sykes of rock'n'roll, and we just didn't have the heart to see them traipse all the way back to Newton Aycliffe without having played a note. Perhaps we should have done. Like a lot of cracking bands, Freddy and the Fire Balls underwent a complete transformation the moment they stepped out on stage. The four nasally challenged brats who'd called at the caravan door to ask if they could have their ball back instantly became lean, leather-clad renegades dispatching supercharged punked-up rock'n'roll classic after classic while pulling poses Gene Vincent would have died for. (Actually, Gene Vincent died in 1971 of a burst stomach ulcer, but you know what I'm saying.) The crowd, already loving it, practically orgasmed as one when, in the closing stages of their last number, Ball played my (Chinny's) Slingerland standing on the drum stool, while Fire tossed Les's guitar high into the air and Freddy scaled the lighting scaffold and crossed over the band thirty feet above the stage. The bass player didn't move much, but then, much to the relief of Wammo, who'd lent him his brand-new bass, they never do.

The cheers of the audience as the band left the stage were deafening, and the same collective thought must have been circulating the arena: 'If Freddy and the Fire Balls were as good as that, then how good must "the most blistering live band in Britain" be?'

Backstage, the most blistering live band in Britain were doing a passable impression of the most shit-scared live band in Holland.

'Little Geordie bastards.'

'Did you see what he did with my guitar?'

'Christ, we're in it up to our necks here, lads,' I mused helpfully.

Wammo didn't say much, which meant he was either smashed out of his brains or, in an admirable example of method acting, was taking this bass player lark very seriously indeed.

Des decided to stall for time, working on the reasonable assumption that we wouldn't compare so unfavourably if the memory of Freddy and the Fire Balls wasn't quite so fresh. There was always the risk, of course, that the crowd would grow increasingly restless with each passing minute and would accordingly expect the most blistering live band in Britain to be even more blistering than usual. Normally, an impatient audience can be calmed for a while by the sight of pot-bellied roadies in Blue Oyster Cult T-shirts trudging across the stage with torches, gaffer–taping cables to the floor. As our equipment was already set up on stage, we didn't have this option open to us, although we did bribe a stage-hand to fanny about with towels and bottles of water in full view of the crowd to buy Phil a few precious extra minutes of lavatory time. Eventually, we ran out of fictitious excuses and accepted that the time had come to put our heads above the parapet. As we sloped across the backstage enclosure towards the platform on which the public execution was to take place, and as the compère's rabid introduction repeated our 'blistering' boast, the vindictive precipitation divinity decided to wreak his last act of vengeance and dispatched a light but steady drizzle over the Groningen area. You would have to say that the omens were not good.

As we strode out on to the stage attempting to look like we meant business, I had cause once again to be grateful that I was the drummer. Stuck away at the back, I was not only far enough from the front rows to avoid eye contact, but safely out of the rain under the protection of the overhead canopy. In his dual role as bassist and babysitter for the drummer, Phil nestled gratefully in the gathering shadows at the rear of the stage and, nodding towards Des and Les, said, 'Bloody hell, I wish we weren't here, but at least we're not on the front line with those two.'

Des, recognising that there is no hiding-place for lead singers on occasions like these, grabbed the microphone and, thrusting his chiselled, grizzled features into the squall, shouted, 'Right then, Groningen, do you feel good?'

As a question, it was better left rhetorical, because with the rain falling steadily and Freddy and the Fire Balls but a distant memory, the response was less than enthusiastic. Evidently, Groningen did not feel good at all, thank you very much. However, they were about to feel a good deal worse. Des turned to face Wammo and, with a look of blind terror, hissed, 'Hell's teeth – let's get this over with.'

I consoled myself in the knowledge that at least the first song, whatever it was called, wasn't half bad and perhaps, just perhaps, it would put the crowd in a good enough mood to accept the rest of the set. Les Bartlett gave his false front teeth a last securing push and, with four sound stomps of his bricklayer's jackboot, launched into his opening riff.

If he'd been loud in rehearsal, he was absolutely deafening now, and to say it took the audience by surprise would be an understatement. Some of them were almost as gobsmacked as the rest of the band. I've heard quieter anti-aircraft guns. The massive distortion that accompanied this cacophony rendered all notes and chords unrecognisable, and whatever it was he was playing, it sounded nothing like what we'd rehearsed for all of half an hour in a leaky Nissen hut back in Poulton. The only conclusion I could draw from the searing white noise attacking my ear-drums was that they'd changed the order of the songs and not bothered to tell me. In fairness, it's often not worth telling the drummer what songs you're playing, because the titles won't mean anything to him anyway, but the opening song was the only one I knew, the only one where I could demonstrate to the sidestage conglomeration of the drummers out of Smokey Sam and Big Bill's respective blues bands and Ball out of Freddy and the Fire Balls that I really could leather that Slingerland with the best of them. As it was, I was reduced to lip-reading Wammo, who, back to the audience and positioned directly in front of the drums, attempted to impose some sort of loose structure on proceedings. How Des was coping, I really couldn't say, due on the one hand to the inferior sound mix and on the other to Les, who couldn't have been making more noise if he'd strapped on a small jet engine. Throughout the gig I never heard any vocals at all, which at least was consistent with the rehearsal. I was pretty shaky as it was, and suddenly hearing the vocals would have cast me hopelessly adrift. Between songs, though, I was able to experience the full effect of Des's charismatic announcements, which were: 'Holland, let's rip it up.' (Holland preferred 'it' untorn.) 'All right, let's shake this place to its foundations.' (Hardly appropriate in a field, where foundations are rarely to be found.) 'This is our new single.' (We did not have a single, new or otherwise.) And 'Come on, you bastards, *clap*.' (The 'bastards' had developed applause fatigue.)

I won't bore you by describing the rest of the songs we played that night, and perhaps we should have spared the audience the boredom of listening to them. Suffice to say that they all sounded exactly the same: bass, drums and vocals struggling to be heard over Les Bartlett's art-rock terrorist assault. As we left the stage to a smattering of appreciative whistles, we encountered representatives of most of the other bands who'd appeared that day. Astonishingly, many of them proffered their hands and expressed admiration at the energy of our performance, which meant that they were, in that peculiar Dutch way, either addicted to cordiality or stoned out of their minds, and quite possibly both. You have to remember that these were people who'd been playing 'Smokestack Lightnin' for thirty-five years, not out of a deep love of the blues, but because they were too out of their trees to play anything else and too deferential to each other to suggest anything different. Unexpectedly, the promoter was extravagantly enthusiastic about our 'show', as he inexplicably referred to it, and gleefully announced that he'd handed over the full fee to Mr Quimby. Others backstage were less forthcoming in their praise, although the head of security, inordinately courteous for a jumped-up bouncer, thanked us for dispersing the crowd in dribs and drabs, therefore averting a crush at the exists. Naturally, being Dutch, the indigenous population spoke much better English than we did, but as we left the site we could see gaggles of mud-caked unfortunates reading the posters to try and ascertain the true meaning of the word 'blistering', which had patently lost something in translation.

We headed for the ferry terminal in convoy; two roadies, the band and the equipment in the van following Jimmy Quimby's Cortina Ghia, which contained the eminent Mr Q along with his recently and mysteriously arrived wife.

There was no sign of Eric Clapton, though. The journey home was largely uneventful, and in truth our mood was relatively buoyant, not only because we were glad it was all over, but also because we'd fully expected to be beaten to a pulp by incandescent Europeans demanding a full refund and private medical treatment.

At the docks, vans and cars were forced into separate queues and so we lost sight of Jimmy Quimby, who had already planned for this eventuality by arranging to meet in the bar once we had set sail. Sitting in Captain Barnacle's Lagoon Saloon, we reflected on the past few days:

'Christ almighty, I don't know how we got away with that.'

'Yeah, it's a good job they're used to bobbins bands over there.'

'Remind me never to play again, ever.'

'Has anyone seen my teeth?'

It was only after an hour or so of such compelling conversation that we began to sense that all was not well. Where was Jimmy Quimby and, more to the point, where was our money? Whether the great impresario would ever have paid us on board as promised, we never had a chance to find out, due to the fact that he never made it on to that particular crossing on account of the bags of speed that were found in the boot of his car. The drive back up north to home soil was accordingly a sullen affair, particularly as Brian and Bendy, the roadies, had had to accept that there would be no pay cheque at the end of three days of rain, noise and stolen food. To their eternal credit, they didn't just dump us as soon as we docked in Sheerness, but out of the goodness of their hearts, and seeing that our plight was every bit as bad as theirs, drove us to the outskirts of Manchester before dumping us on the hard shoulder. Obviously we couldn't carry the drum-kit, but they promised to look after it until we could collect it. Needless to say, we never saw that Slingerland again, and I can only assume they took it in lieu of wages.

Guitars in hand and empty of pocket, we had no alternative but to embark on a six-mile trudge through the breaking half-light of dawn back to the Booth Avenue hovel.

'Hey, Phil, at least there's one thing to be grateful for.'

'Oh yeah, and what's that, then?'

'My boots have dried out.'

7

Bob Sleigh and the Crestas

The aftermath of the Holland débâcle proved to be a testing time. On arriving back at our flat, everyone made themselves uncomfortable on a stuffing-spewing settee or damp divan to grab some much-needed sleep. Rising around tea-time, it immediately became apparent that me and my girlfriend, who in the interests of protecting her identity we'll call Sara and not her real name, which is Sally Medlock, had a problem on our hands. After feeding them sumptuously on crumpets, button burgers and alphabetti spaghetti, we considered our charitable work manning a soup kitchen for the Fylde's down-and-outs to be over, and, as they showed no sign of moving on, began to drop mild hints into the conversation. Stretching prodigiously, I said, 'Blimey heckers, this trip's taken it out of me big style. I think I'll be back to my pit soon.'

'Yeah, me, too,' murmured Des, barely taking his eyes off a particularly engrossing edition of *Opportunity Knocks*.

'I'll bet you'll be glad to get back to Poulton, then,' offered Sara.

'No rush,' said Les Bartlett. 'Gran'll have watered my conker trees.'

'Yes, but there's nothing like sleeping in your own bed, is there?' I pleaded.

'You're right there, Sparky,' chimed Wammo. 'I suppose my old bed's still where it was?'

'Yes, with the same sheets still on it. I would have changed them, but I haven't got round to borrowing a hammer and chisel.'

As the evening wore on and *Opportunity Knocks* gave way to *Coronation Street*, a folk opera set in considerably more luxurious surroundings than the ones we found ourselves in, it became obvious that our gentle suggestions were having no discernible effect. I decided to take a less subtle course of action.

'Right, lads, you've had a kip, we've fed you and let you dry off your underpants on the gas fire, and now I'd be obliged if you'd all piss off.'

'Ah, well, there's a bit of a problem there, Mark.'

Thanks to Jimmy Quimby, we'd come back without a penny, and as Sara and I were, as was the prevailing fashion at the time, students on the dole, we did not have the means to finance return travel to Poulton-le-Fylde for these three stooges, by which I mean the badly dressed, improbably coiffured, distinctly unfunny film pillocks Curly, Larry and Mo, and not the drop-dead-cool backing band of Iggy Pop. There was nothing we could do. We couldn't put them out on the streets – the other dossers would have complained about the smell. We would just have to put them up for two or three days until the next giro cheques came through.

Re-ensconced in his old environs, Wammo noticed with some disapproval the changes that had been made in his absence.

'Oi, what's happened to the fungus I grew on the kitchen wall? It took me ages to nurture that, and now someone's scraped it all off.'

'A woman's touch, Wammo, a woman's touch.'

Those few days seemed like an eternity as Des spent long hours in front of the telly doing a passable impersonation of a bean-bag, and Wammo spent long hours in the bathroom evacuating his bowels. I've come across many men who spend inordinate lengths of time engrossed in the art of defecation, but Phil was in a league of his own. It's quite common for people to retire to the privacy of the water-closet with a newspaper, but he went in there with the *New Musical Express*, a copy of *International Musician* magazine, a biography of Keith Richard, a large mug of tea and a Tupperware box of meat-paste sandwiches. He packed more stuff to go for a poo than he did to go to Holland. The genial Les Bartlett had no annoying habits at all, apart from leaving his dental plate lying about on the kitchen worktops so you'd inadvertently put your hand on it just before dining handsomely on potato cakes and pot noddle. It curbed your appetite, I can tell you.

Eventually dole day came around and we gleefully handed over the cash for the train fares. It meant a week living on Cup-A-Soup, but it was worth it.

Astonishingly, the sorry Skrewdriver story didn't end there. Don't ask me why, but I went back on the road to do a few gigs to unsurprisingly small but mystifyingly enthusiastic audiences at premier-league rock venues like the Leeds Fforde Green Hotel, the Manchester Mayflower, the Digbeth Turdbowl and the Dumfries Stagecoach; this despite Des's insistence that he didn't want to play in any 'out-of-the-way places like . . . Scotland'.

Mark Radcliffe

It's strange thing about being in a band that you are simultaneously drawn together while finding the prospect totally repellent. Between the spells of not speaking to each other and beating the bass player senseless, there are periods of camaraderie and good humour that are utterly addictive, and every so often you need to top yourself up. The gig that convinced me to go into detox took place at another venue that has since become what you might call legendary if you were an inveterate liar: the Golden Diamond Club, Sutton in Ashfield.

Sutton in Ashfield is approximately sixty miles from Manchester, and on a bad day it can take you two hours to drive there, should you feel the compulsion to do so, which is distinctly unlikely. Despite its comparative proximity, we managed, through a combination of misfortune and incompetence, to make the round trip last close on forty-eight hours. The promoter was a breed we'd not encountered before in that he seemed intent on leaving himself broke as well as the band.

'I'm sorry, lads, but I've completely forgotten to advertise the gig at all,' he announced cheerfully. 'But don't worry, I'll let you have one hundred per cent of the door takings.'

This sounded more than fair under the circumstances, although we had no way of knowing that the number of people who would cough up the seventy-five-pence admission charge would be three. There were four of us in the band, three roadies with the PA and a van driver, which meant that on a straight eight-way split we could look forward to a reward for our labours of around twenty-eight pence each.

Later in the evening this alleged promoter, a charitable

134

fellow unlikely ever to become a close associate of Harvey Goldsmith, gallantly offered everyone free beer. In retrospect, he probably considered his kindness ill-judged. We eventually staggered on to the stage around midnight, blind drunk, and proceeded to produce the most unpleasant sound it was possible to hear, not counting a Whitesnake concert. Some hours later, the exasperated landlord pulled the plugs and called the police to eject us from the premises. Loading PA cabinets and drum-kits into a van by police flashlight at three o'clock in the morning on a God-forsaken windswept mudflat in Sutton in Ashfield may not sound like much fun, but, to be honest, we were too bladdered to care.

'Right, then,' boomed one stout representative of the local constabulary, 'and who's the driver?'

'He's sleeping off a skinful in the toilets, Officer,' said Wammo helpfully.

'So there's not one of you who's under the limit, then?'

'There's not one of us who can remember what the limit is, Constable.'

With a heavy sigh, the two policemen conferred before loading us all on to the van, driving us to the county border and dumping us in a lay-by in the middle of nowhere. For the second time in recent memory I was stranded, penniless, on the hard shoulder with a bunch of imbeciles who would struggle to put on a new pair of Y-fronts without reading the instructions first. That was the straw that broke the donkey's jaw-bone, and when we got back I told Wammo in no uncertain terms that I'd had enough.

'I've had enough,' I said.

'Those sound like no uncertain terms,' said Wammo.

*   *   *

I didn't see Phil for the rest of that summer, but when he returned in the autumn we went to a gig which provided the inspiration for our next doomed stab at the big time, although we'd have happily settled for a stab at the medium time, it being one step up from the small time. We'd heard about a sound coming out of Coventry under the auspices of an independent label called 2-tone. Bands like the Specials, Selecter and Madness, who we subsequently discovered came from London, were repopularising ska and blue beat played with all the attack of punk. In many ways it was an inevitable development, as all the new-wave gigs we'd attended had throbbed to a soundtrack of dub reggae, and the natural outcome of a culture clash of Culture and the Clash was new ska. The three principal exponents of the revitalised genre were selling out venues across the country on their package tour, so it was with a sense of some anticipation that we entered the Manchester Apollo that night.

Selecter came on first, and we were immediately impressed by the suits. They wore tight tonic two-pieces in shimmering mohair, even lead singer Pauline Black, topped off with sunglasses and pork pie hats. Phil, in particular, was much taken with the concept of the headgear and enthusiastically suggested a beat combo called the Pork Pie Hats, for which each member would wear the crust of a large catering pork pie on his or her head, pausing between numbers to wipe the marrowbone jelly from their eyes. What a visionary that boy was. The band didn't seem abundantly blessed with great songs, although 'Too Much Pressure' and 'On My Radio' stick in the memory, but the rhythm in conjunction with the sight of seven band members running on the spot proved hugely seductive. It seems to me that, when sampled live, ska is like Cajun: if you don't dance, then you're dead from the neck down.

After a short break Madness came on, and any last vestiges of scepticism melted away as the nutty boys converted us lock, stock and double-barrel to the ska faith. In truth, Madness would have succeeded in any era, being a sublime synthesis of punk, reggae, music hall and classic English pop. Their songs, in those days largely the work of pianist Mike Barson, owed as much to Ray Davies as Joe Strummer, and sound as effortless and wonderful today as they did when first released. From their ska roots they went from strength to strength with a sequence of timeless singles, including 'Baggy Trousers', 'Embarrassment', 'Grey Day', 'Our House', and one of the truly great pop records of all time, 'House of Fun'. In their later years they became, like ageing clowns, darker in their outlook. They released more sombre singles like 'One Better Day' and 'Yesterday's Men', and dressed in black frock-coats as if they'd become a sublime synthesis of punk, reggae, music hall, classic English pop and a firm of down-at-heel undertakers. That night at the Apollo, though, it was all irresistible ska showpieces, including 'The Prince', a tribute to trail-blazer Prince Buster, 'One Step Beyond', 'Night Boat to Cairo' and their celebrated stab at *Swan Lake*, during which Tchaikovsky may well have been rotating in his tomb, but if he was, he was doing it in a series of rhythmic jerks. The rhythmic jerks on stage were a joy to behold. They had a bloke called Chas Smash, who has become the most celebrated Bez in pop apart from Bez himself. His job was to dance next to singer Suggs like a man possessed, or a man in fear of being busted for possession, cruise up to the microphone

occasionally and from beneath the brim of his pork pie hat
emit a string of clenched-teeth 'chikka-chikka-chikka-chikka'
noises interspersed with the odd 'oi'. What a splendid chap.
At regular intervals he would lead the band in a single-file
crocodile across the stage, demonstrating the trademark
slow-motion staccato-sprinting Madness dance, which Phil
and I would later perform halfway along Hyde Road until
we found a kebab house. The great thing about Madness
was that they exuded good humour, like they were just a
bunch of mates out for a laugh. They took the music a lot
more seriously than they took themselves, and that was what
endeared them to a generation of fans.

Championship contenders the Specials were on last and
demonstrated the same energy and commitment as Selecter,
with songs almost on a par with Madness, but without the
unrelenting sense of fun. Specials vocalist Terry Hall is a man
of mournful countenance concealing, as I now know through
my show-business connections, a wicked sense of humour,
but back then we'd had enough glum attitude during the
punk wars and were looking for some light relief. Under their
general, Jerry Dammers, they were generally more political
than Madness, and would themselves come to produce a
cache of towering singles, articulating what it was like to
be young, unemployed and a victim of racism in the Little
Britain of the late seventies and early eighties. Songs like
'Too Much Too Young', 'Rat Race' and 'Stereotypes' struck
a chord with the disenfranchised as punk had done three years
previously. By far the greatest Specials single, though, was
'Ghost Town', where the deadpan Hall intoned the words:

This town is coming like a ghost town,

All the clubs have been closed down.
This place is coming like a ghost town,
Bands don't play no more,
Too much fighting on the dance floor . . .

against a backdrop of disembodied sirens and slack ska
menace. Released in 1981 as inner-city riots swept the
nation, it remains as much a snapshot of those times as
any news footage.

In the days that followed the gig, Wammo and I began
to hatch plans to become Manchester's answer to Madness.
We figured we had the stupidity in the bank already and
just needed to take out a loan on some good songs. We
couldn't run to mohair suits, but we dusted off our narrow,
single-breasted Dr Feelgood Oxfam outfits, which we began
to wear daily, although the look was let down by the
footwear. The baseball boots had long since rotted and had
been replaced with a now defunct type of shoe known as
the Nature Trek. These consisted of a moulded rubber soul
with no instep, on top of which a single piece of leather had
been doubled over, resulting in a seam running across your
toes and down one side, while the other side was simply a
fold. You looked like you had Cornish pasties on your feet.
The essence of mod cool they weren't.

The next thing we needed was a band, and a big one.
One of the things all the 2-tone acts had in common was
that there were hundreds of people leaping about on stage
singing, playing guitar, blowing into a saxophone or acting
the twonk for no apparent reason. We decided to recruit
everyone we knew who could play anything, and some who
couldn't play at all but who we thought looked funny.

'It'll be brilliant,' said Phil, 'like getting all your family together and going on holiday.'

Well, I knew what he meant, but getting your whole family together to go on holiday is often a recipe for disaster. Think about it. All year you live with your nearest and occasionally dearest in a house with a variety of rooms with different designated purposes. At the same time, different family members can watch television in the living-room, listen to the radio and have a cup of tea and a fag in the kitchen, or play loud music to conceal the grunts of adolescent love-making in the bedroom. On top of this, there are further distractions such as video games, telephones, guitars and painting-by-numbers, all designed to keep families out of each other's hair. Then once a year, for a treat, the whole brood moves into one room in a semi-built self-catering breeze-block prison camp in Tossa de Mar. It's a wonder they don't kill each other.

Shockingly, some parents are even more cruel that that, forcing their offspring to spend valuable holiday time in tents or caravans. Do social services know about this? Don't get me wrong, there are circumstances in which living under canvas is perfectly acceptable, if you are an essentially nomadic people like the Bedouin, for example, or if your house has been demolished by a freak tidal wave. Otherwise forget it. Of course, seasoned campers will try and persuade you of the benefits of their deranged activity: 'Aah, well, tents are better than they were, you know. Ours has got its own chemical toilet.' Brilliant. We all know that passing solid waste produces a distinctly unpleasant aroma and a variety of straining and splashing sounds which are best left unheard except by the defecator. Why anyone would want to perform this process behind a flimsy awning, silhouetted by the light of a storm lantern, is a mystery to me. I'll say one thing for campers, though, at least their tents don't clog up the roads, which is more than you can say for caravanners. You will already have encountered a beginner's guide to caravan accessories in Chapter 5, but what of caravanning on the open highway? Why they think the rest of us should travel at ten miles an hour as they negotiate their twenty-five-foot cool box on wheels round the approach to Corfe Castle, I really can't imagine. I fully believe that caravans should be kept off the road by day, and burnt at night. The arrogance of these people is quite staggering. Why should we be forced to crawl along country lanes behind some bloke who's too mean to check his family into a guest-house? The humble snail moves slowly with its home in tow, but I think most of us would like to believe we'd worked our way a bit further up the evolutionary scale than that.

The recruitment drive to fill the ranks began in earnest. Friends and acquaintances fell over themselves to hitch a ride on our latest bandwagon. Well, if I'm perfectly honest, most of them fell over themselves because they'd hit the Scrumpy Jack too early, and those that didn't, fell over themselves because they lacked the necessary co-ordination to walk effectively.

I'd been playing organ in a band called the Brilliantines, which was either a post-modern deconstructivist co-operative or a load of old toss, depending on your point of view. As this book is exclusively concerned with bands who have had a major impact on the twentieth-century Western pop *oeuvre*, the Brilliantines need not concern us here, but my fellow crypto-situationist art-rock pioneers were among the first to sign up to the blue-beat big band.

There was our old mate Stig Burgess from Bolton, who agreed to ditch his guitar and concentrate on harmonica. Then there was Baz Ilott, the world's most unreliable bassist, and there can't be many more hotly contested mantles than that. Baz was a bluff Yorkshireman who'd managed to get himself elected to the sabbatical post of social secretary of the student union. This was, of course, at a time when students were still possessed of a revolutionary fervour and, in an attempt to destabilise institutions from within, filled key union posts with whichever candidate was likely to prove most inept. We liked Baz a lot, and he was a reasonable bass player, but I won't deny that we cultivated his acquaintance because we thought if we couldn't get gigs on merit, then it was as well to have the promoter in the band. On drums was a bloke we knew from the poly called Jerome Ballinger. He was known to everyone as J. G. Giant on account of his considerable size, his constant good humour and his ever-present green pullover, which reminded us of the celebrated jolly green giant of golden-niblets-of-corn television-advertisement fame. One of the essential ingredients of the ska sound was the saxophone, so that meant a return on a free transfer from teacher-training for former Zeroid Paul Hemingway, and we also swooped on the chubby and genial rhythm guitarist Jack 'Mad Axe' Carlton, whose previous band had set Wigan alight, although he always contested the forensic evidence. Next came two friends of Baz's called Flash and Mac McMahon. Flash was perhaps the finest jew's harpist in the department of sociology, and also had the snappiest suit and crop of all of us. He had also managed to retain a perennially youthful air, thanks mainly to the preservation of his pubescent acne. Mac McMahon, known to everyone as Pifco on account of the incident with the torch, was a computer science deserter and major-league pisshead from Belfast who was recruited on percussion, which as often as not meant taking two lump hammers to a double-drainer sink. Completing the line-up were Stig's tap-dancing girlfriend Looby and our next-door neighbour Dougie Somerfield, who was a drummer of some renown. We already had the Giant signed up as drummer, but we figured it was probably worth having a spare. In fact, there was even a third drummer called Bernie, who we called upon in times of crisis along with tentative trumpeter Chambo, a kilt-wearing white-Rasta electrician from Handforth.

Often there were so many people turning up to play that not everyone got a gig, which is one of the frustrations of the deep-squad system, but as Ruud Gullit and I both know, it's much easier to keep players on their toes if there's someone warming up to fill their position. In truth, I don't know why more bands don't operate a squad system. If you go and see Pink Floyd or Dire Straits in a football stadium, you've no idea who's up there anyway, so the manager could select his formation on the team bus and switch things around at half-time if it's not going too well, which admittedly with Dire Straits would be pretty much every gig. Think of the advantages, though, of a stage-side bench of hungry young products of the youth policy, solid centre-back bass players and flighty lead-guitar wingers ready to come on if the old retainers drop a howler or pull up with a strained hamstring incurred while executing an ambitious scissor-kick. If I was the Spice Girls' manager you'd probably never have heard of them, but I'd be tempted to recruit a few reserves so that if Sporty had to go off following an awkward backflip landing, you could bring on either Sprightly Spice or Spunky Spice, who'd been limbering up in the wings. Of course, in the case of our particular squad we had so many undisciplined mavericks on the books that we were more likely to resemble Everton than Ajax, but I still believe in the basic principle.

There were also a couple of other people who appeared from time to time whose names I never knew. I was in a crowded bar a couple of years ago when a bloke tapped me on the shoulder and said, 'What are you doing drinking my pint?' Shortly after that, another bloke tapped me on the shoulder and said, 'It's Mark, isn't it?'

Never to my knowledge having seen him before, I hesitantly confirmed my Christian name, but could see my reaction was not what he'd expected.

'You don't remember me, do you?' he said, crestfallen.

'I'm sorry, I don't. Should I?'

'We were in a band together.'

'Were we? Which one?'

'That ska band.'

'Really? What position did you play?'

'I was on the right flank, next to the tap-dancer, overlapping the bloke hitting the sink.'

'Aah, well, no wonder I don't recognise you, I never used to go over that side much.'

This was true. The midfield ranks were often so crowded that dribbling across the full width of the stage proved impossible for those without the balance of Gio Kinkladze.

'Well, I'm really sorry I forgot you. What was your role in the band?'

'I was the one who sat on stage reading a newspaper,' he announced gleefully, and I had to admit that he did ring some vague bells, or was that someone else again? Had we really had a campanologist on board?

So the definitive line-up was in place: guitar, bass, drums, organ, sax, trumpet, jew's harp, drums, guitar, harmonica, dance (tap), percussion (mixer tap), newspaper and er . . . drums. All we needed now was a name.

As I recall, the naming of the band was left to the inner sanctum of Wammo, Stig and I. We all agreed that it had to be a name in the fine sixties tradition of a front man and his backing group, like Brian Poole and the Tremoloes, Freddie and the Dreamers, Gerry and the Pacemakers, or Ringo and the Beatles. There were even contemporary examples in Johnny Thunders and the Heartbreakers, Siouxsie and the Banshees and, not least, Echo and the Bunnymen (which led many people to assume that lead singer Ian McCulloch would be more likely to respond if addressed with the formal greeting, 'Oi, Echo!'). The idea of a fictitious front man appealed to us, as it would not only add confusion to the audience's existing irritation, but also avoid any power struggles within the ranks. We were all the best of mates, but if anyone had tried to secure star billing for himself we'd have calmly explained to him the error of his ways before smacking him on the back on the neck with one of J. G. Giant's baseball bat drumsticks. It may well have been the knock on the head that led Stig to come up with the name Bob Sleigh and the Crestas. The moment he said it, we knew it was perfect, but that didn't stop us coming up with a list of alternatives involving a series of similarly weak puns: Max Headroom and the Low Bridges, Barry Tone and the Tenors, Stevie Dore and the Dockers, Derrick Oil and the Drillers, Al Pine and the Glaciers, Duncan Disorderly and His Pissed-Up Farts all being considered for approximately the length of time it took to sink a pint.

Against all the odds, our first gig proved something of a triumph. We were booked to play at the Manchester University Fresher's Ball, supporting not only the great lost punk-pop band the Distractions, but also the notorious oven-ready leader of the pot-bellied gang himself, Mr Gary Glitter. When I say we were booked, I mean our bass player just added us to the bill without telling anyone, a blatant abuse of his official position which made Wammo and I glow with a certain paternalistic pride. We'd recruited Baz sensing that he had the potential for wanton misuse of elected office, and he was already paying back the faith we'd shown in him.

We opened with a particularly fiery ska rendition of the old scouting classic 'Ging Gang Gooly', before sliding seamlessly into the theme tune from *The Magnificent Seven*, which in turn gave way to a blue beat bombardment of Sandie Shaw's seminal 'Puppet on a String'. Paul Hemingway's subtle and ingenious saxophone-as-penis-substitute show-case 'Too Much Sax' proved a real crowd pleaser, as did the first fruits of the fledgling songwriting partnership of Sparky/Giant: 'Cresta Rap' and 'New Red Shoes'. The latter was inspired by the impoverished Brobdingnagian's dubious purchase from the bargain bins at Freeman, Hardy & Willis, an acquisition made for financial rather than stylistic reasons. A pair of crimson, crepe-soled coal barges is a perfectly acceptable form of footwear, for the under-fives. In adult size twelve they were a hazard to traffic. Of course, while writing a song about shoes could be readily dismissed as the drunken ramblings of middle-class college boys with far too much time on their hands, it's easy to overlook the allegorical implications of a couplet like 'I bought them in the summer sales, And now my feet are like beached red whales', where the selfsame shoes become a metaphor for the downtrodden specimens left stranded by a cynical society. Similarly 'Cresta Rap', a meticulous parody, not of American street culture, but of Adam and the Ants' 'Ant Rap', had a lyrical complexity that extended to the back of a second beer-mat. A ska-tological reworking of Tom Jones's 'Delilah' came next, the violent central image of the 'knife in his hand' being replaced with a pacifist pie, before a medley of several Western cinema classics took us to our grand finale. This took the form of an homage to the great televisual variety institution of *Sunday Night at the London Palladium*, where the cream of the world's light-entertainment talent would bring the show to a fitting climax by waving to the rapturous crowds from a revolving stage. We didn't have a revolving stage, but we recreated the effect by standing shoulder to shoulder, instruments in hand, and shuffling in a clockwise direction while hammering the immortal strains of the *Palladium* signature tune. For guitarists, saxophonists and tap-dancers, this choreographic conclusion proved relatively straightforward. For drummers, organists and plumbed-in percussionists, the process proved considerably more taxing, resulting in a spaghetti-like tangle of cables, microphones and stands that resulted in a forty-five-minute delay to the appearance of the Distractions. The new influx of spotty students, spirited along by cheap beer and their first taste of freedom, loved every minute of it. We might even have

147

done an encore, had we had another song and had we not rendered the stage unusable.

Over the next three terms we appeared regularly in clubs, colleges and halls of residence using equipment bought with union funds intended to replace the antiquated disco and sound system in the cellar bar. Improbable as it might seem, demand for our services became so great that we once accepted two bookings on the same night. Wammo and I seriously considered fielding two completely different line-ups who could play simultaneously in separate venues, giving members of our youth squad some much-needed first-team experience. Eventually we rejected this policy on the grounds that both venues would provide us with free beer and we wanted to be there to drink it.

The first gig of the evening passed without incident at a city-centre night-spot known as the Gallery. By this time we'd extended our performance to include several cameo support acts selected from the massed Cresta ranks. Often a busking contingent of three or four members would be selected either by drawing names from a hat, usually a fez, or by having their fingers bent back until they acquiesced. This advance party would then be sent out on to the pavement outside the venue to attract passing casual trade or to send it scurrying across the street, depending on the instrumentation deployed and the level of inebriation of its operatives. At college venues we would commandeer the security lodge and perform a tantalising taster set through the tannoy system. We also provided a succession of novelty attractions, which on this occasion included 'J. G. Giant's Your Hundred Best Tunes' (which involved rolling around on-stage with a drum and a cymbal screaming 'The hills are alive with the sound of music'), 'Wammo's Shadow Puppet Theatre' (which involved rolling around on-stage behind a back-lit and worryingly stained bed sheet), and 'Flash and Pifco's Folk Dance Forum' (which involved rolling around on-stage beating each other with bottle-top-embellished broom handles). All this for the price of one band. What a bargain.

You don't get that sort of value for money these days. A lot of today's top bands are really quite proficient, but that doesn't mean their live shows couldn't be jazzed up with a full supporting variety show. Wouldn't it be nice to see Bonehead and Guigsy doing a little puppetry for the kids before Oasis came on? Don't loyal Radiohead fans deserve the chance to see a blindfolded Jonny Greenwood throwing steak knives at a revolving Thom Yorke? Instead of lounging about backstage like a load of big girls' blouses, why don't the Verve take two clean handkerchiefs each and show us they're no slouches in the Morris-dancing stakes? 'And now, ladies and gentlemen, Michael Bolton will demonstrate his expertise in the oriental art of origami.' Well, anything that stops the bastard singing has got to be a bonus. Today's pop stars just don't know what hard work is, but then everything's changed since I was a lad. I can still remember the Glastonbury Festival site when it was all fields.

Having completed engagement number one, we made hasty arrangements to tackle the evening's second appointment. The web of intertwined leads, instruments and DIY accessories that lay centre-stage was tossed into the back of the mini-van owned and driven by the ferret-like leader of the drum corps, Dougie Somerfield. Dougie was a somewhat isolated figure on account of being teetotal. Having a member of the band who doesn't drink is very handy when it comes to getting from gig to gig, but they don't tend to stay around for long. Generally, to use a series of liquid images, they quickly tire of the streams of verbal abuse, the spurts of sporadic fisticuffs and the pools of vomit left on their vehicular upholstery. With the equipment safely in transit, the rest of us set about ordering taxis to transport us to the next theatre of dreams. Naturally, it being Saturday night, this proved problematic. Why are minicab companies staffed entirely by pathological liars?

'Hello, cab at the Gallery, please. How long will that be?'

'Five minutes, mate. What's the name?'

This from a man who knows full well he hasn't got a hope in hell of picking you up for another forty-five minutes, and then only in a Y-reg Datsun MOT failure driven by a corpulent bigot with BO chain-smoking Superkings.

Inevitably, this leads to you phoning again twenty minutes after your initial call to be told that 'the driver'll be with you in two minutes, he's just around the corner'. Well, fancy that. Despite being only yards away, however, the driver, obviously keen to cause the prospective passenger maximum irritation, manages to achieve speeds so low that arrival from 'just around the corner' still takes up to half an hour. I don't know who it was who said that time is an abstract concept, but they'd obviously worked for a minicab firm.

The second booking of the night was at a large pub in south Manchester, where a local amateur football club had booked a large function room in which to hold its annual awards evening. Mid-ceremony, when we made our belated arrival, the assembled pack of Sunday league bullet-heads and their respective candyfloss-haired bimbettes did not take kindly to the invasion of amply lubricated student types carrying, among other things, a stainless-steel sink. Directed to the far end of the dance floor, we began to unpack our instruments of torture, filling the entire width of the room in the process. Behind us, against the wall, was a buffet laid out with every manner of food you could think of if you were particularly unimaginative in matters culinary. What it lacked in creativity, though, it more than made up for in quantity. There were enough egg fingers, Scotch eggs and pork pies on that table to feed a squad of overweight, pug-faced soccer psychopaths, which was just as well under the circumstances. Surveying the clientele, we decided to forgo the warm-up acts. We predicted we were going to have trouble getting away with the main set as it was, but, bladdered as we were, we could see that if confronted by Phil in his underpants doing 'Man being eaten by crocodile' behind a grubby tablecloth, the crowd were liable to turn very ugly. Most of them were halfway there already.

As we launched into 'Ging Gang Gooly' for the second time that night, it became immediately apparent, even more so than usual, that something was wrong. Dougie, being stone-cold sober and therefore quicker off the mark, identified the problem straight away: 'Where the hell is Paul?'

'Jesus Christ, I thought he was in the van with you.'

'No, you tosser, you said he was going in your cab.'

Whoever's fault it was, the end result was that our esteemed saxophonist had been left stranded in Manchester with no idea where the second gig was taking place. This proved catastrophic during 'Too Much Sax', which was hurriedly rewritten as 'Too Much Organ', but it just wasn't

Mark Radcliffe

the same. The already depleted sound was also plagued by
a continuous low growl. Further investigation identified the
source of this bowel-loosening rumble as Baz's bass, propped
up against his amplifier while the absent social secretary sated
his appetite at the otherwise untouched buffet. I think we'd
have got away with even this, had not the part of 'Delilah'
containing the words 'I saw the pie in his hand' been dramatically embellished by the hurling of a Holland's meat beauty,
which caught Jack 'Mad Axe' Carlton a glancing blow on the
back of the head before landing amid the raffle prizes. At this
point I could describe the pitched battle that went on in the
car park following the performance. I could recount how we
were savagely beaten for some considerable length of time
for turning the club's social gathering of the year into a farce.
Sadly, it would all be lies, because the only violence took
place in the lavatories, where a consummate head-butt was
administered to the underweight and undeserving Dougie
Somerfield. Our part-time trumpeter Chambo, who had
made the arrangements through a friend of a friend, quickly
took the club captain's charitable and sensible advice to 'get
these twats out of here before we beat the living shit out of
them'. Some people have no sense of humour, although I
don't think it was the lack of humour that was the problem.
It was more the lack of pies.

The ranks began to get a bit depleted after that. The
line-up was never what you might call stable, but the night
only three of us turned up to play made Phil, Stig and I
realise that the band, always at breaking point, had finally
snapped clean off in several places and was going to need
more than Araldite this time. We never heard from Dougie
again, Chambo had been told in no uncertain terms that he

could seriously damage his health if he was seen out with us on other occasions, and hacked-off Hemingway never forgave us for leaving him that night. J. G. Giant went back to York, where a career in social security fraud and local radio sports reporting awaited him, and Pifco Killerwatt moved to London to live in a Ford Fiesta, eventually becoming a hugely affluent computer magnate.

Still, there were further gigs at the Gallery, where on one notable occasion a double booking had us sharing the stage with a bunch of prog-rockers from Aylesbury. Deciding who should go on first was left to the bands, and so Wammo and I approached their colossal lead singer, who was absorbed in the application of a greasepaint rainbow to his face.

'Hello, we're Mark and Phil.'

'Fish.'

'Sorry?'

'Fish.'

'Fish? What are you on about, pal?'

'My name is Fish.'

'Fair enough, whatever you say, big fella. Now, do you want to go on first or second?'

'Och,' said Fish, who was Scottish, 'we'll go on first because we've got to drive back to Aylesbury.'

And so it came to pass that Bob Sleigh and the Crestas were supported by Marillion, and there aren't many people in showbusiness who can make a boast like that.

8

House on Fire

The illustrious career of Bob Sleigh and the Crestas straddled that crucial watershed in our lives when we ceased being students and stumbled out, blinking, into the bright light of having to work for a living. Neither Wammo nor I has ever made what you might call a wage from music, and there are those who'd wager that we've never made what you might call music, but the Cresta gigs certainly eased the financial pain of a life without grant cheques and subsidised bars. Wammo's intense dedication to the study of house-brick theory, lintel science and gas-fired central heating technology began to pay off as he took his first steps up the ladder of the construction industry. My years of being a pain-in-the-neck hyperactive gobshite also stood me in good stead as I embarked on a working life in radio, first at a local station in Manchester and then at a national station in London with 'One' in its name.

I'd always promised Phil, and myself, that I'd never desert him or the north of England. We'd been through so much together that we knew we'd be mates for the rest of our lives, and if we'd been gay I'm sure we would have got married.

Being strictly heterosexual, our physical relationship remains unconsummated, which I'm sure is as big a relief to him as it is to me. Leaving the frozen wastelands of the north for the playboy rivieras of the south was something I thought I'd never do, but it was one of those opportunities that you just sensed wouldn't present itself again. In a similar moment of infallible intuition, I bought tickets to see the Rolling Stones at Roundhay Park in Leeds, confident that this would be the last time they would perform together as a band. This was 1982, since when they have toured the world four times, although punters paying through the turnstiles these days are denied the full visual feast of the charismatic bassist Bill Wyman, a man who brings a whole new meaning to the adjective 'statuesque'. Off I went, then to seek out the high spots, the fleshpots and the tosspots of the London media circus.

I came back, though.

It was a couple of years down the line, and I was entering that peculiar late twenties time of life when you start to realise you're not eighteen any more, a realisation that dawns on the female of the species on their nineteenth birthday. It's a time when all sorts of peculiar facets of the ageing process become apparent. For the first time since childhood you start to buy clothes at Marks & Spencer. Without actually having made a conscious decision to go there, you find yourself at B & Q considering the relative merits of the Bosch and the Black & Decker power drill, surrounded by a lot of middle-aged people dressed in beige. What did all these people do on a Sunday before the advent of the DIY superstore? You still buy records, but you are now old enough to witness yet another technological breakthrough in recording format, so you repurchase all the albums you first got when you were fourteen on CD DAT minidisc or digitally remastered laser-reissue wax cylinder. Bring back the eight-track cartridge, I say. My own record collection is a considerable one, it being to some degree a tool of my dubious trade, but its size is swelled by the presence of various Led Zeppelin, Bob Dylan, Pink Floyd, Genesis, Nick Drake and Talking Heads albums on several formats each. There's a chain of stores in many city centres called Past Times specialising in gifts evoking memories of bygone eras. You can get things like medieval chess sets, Clarice Cliffe coasters, Edwardian tea cosies and scented Victorian leg-irons. I know I'll have truly become an old man when they start stocking Sex Pistols LPs: 'Relive those innocent Olde Englishe punk rock days of the late 1970s with this luxurious facsimile vinyl edition of *Never Mind the Bollocks.*'

There are the physical manifestations of getting older, too. Ninety per cent of men will apparently experience a gradual thickening of the waistline irrespective of the number of red-faced road miles they pound along the verges of our gridlocked highways. This means that all those hours of unwelcome exercise result only in existing excess poundage being redistributed around the body so that instead of being above the belt-line the belly may eventually come to rest below it, like those eminently large-trousered elders who inhabit crown-green bowling clubs. Of course, you can always take solace from the knowledge that you're a source of huge amusement to passing motorists: 'Hey, kids, look at the funny, sweaty, waddling fat man.' The inevitability of growing pear-shaped might seem a cruel blow dealt to most men by the great feminist matriarch Mother Nature, but in time you may come to look on it as a blessing. You might as well eat and drink what the hell you like if you're going to end up a blob anyway. Imagine how depressing it must be to die with a beer gut after forty years of abstinence.

Apart from the spare tyre there's the hair loss issue to contend with. Strangely enough, the thinning of the thatch on the head experienced by most men is accompanied by an illogical and downright irritating spurt of growth in all areas of the body you'd least like to have hair appear. Personally, I have unwittingly cultivated a sparse but nevertheless unmistakable pubic triangle in the small of my back. I've also noticed that the new hair crop seems to find the sheltered conditions prevalent in my nostrils and ears hugely fertile. I suppose one day I'll be like my grandfather, who for special occasions, while my grandmother was at the hairdresser's having a shampoo and set, would visit the barber's to have his head shaved and his nose trimmed. I've recently seen pictures of a man with eight-inch nasal hairs, and it is truly the most repulsive sight you will ever see. Extraordinarily, this bloke had a loyal and loving wife, which just goes to show that either there's someone for everyone in this world or, worried that there isn't, some women are not too fussy. There are even some who'll sleep with David Mellor.

In many ways I can keep my unwanted pastures under wraps with a little prudent topiary and the refusal to remove my shirt in public, which at least makes me more fortunate than Phil Collins. Poor old Phil's unwanted patch of scrub has had the audacity to appear on the front of his otherwise smooth head. Perhaps it's healthy that bald men like Phil become hugely successful to prove to others that a gleaming pate is no barrier to the ambitious, although I can't imagine there are too many blokes who want to emulate the look of Collins on the cover of his *No Jacket Required* album, where the red lighting has lent him an alarming resemblance to a baked bean.

Naturally, many men who suffer hair loss investigate various ways of concealing the problem. The cheapest of these are aerosol sprays in a range of colours, rather like those available for covering small patches of corrosion on the bodywork of your car, although there aren't many people whose natural hair colour is metallic green. Snooker whirlwind Jimmy White once endorsed such a product in a series of newspaper adverts, explaining how his confidence had returned since he discovered the joys of painting the top of his head. That it works cannot be in doubt; if you can paint over damp patches you can paint over bald ones, and if you're talking large areas you can hire a local painter and decorator to do the work for you. However, it's only ever going to be a temporary measure. Presumably, this was why the same inestimable Mr White appeared in promotional literature some time later extolling the virtues of a revolutionary surgical procedure. As I understand it, this involved slicing the bald area, removing the skin, and bringing the hair at the edges of the cranial crop circle inwards to cover the exposed area. There are several problems I can see with this. One is that if you go in with a short haircut you're going to finish up with the whole lot somewhere above your ears. Another is that there's the possibility of closing the hole in the hair layer only to find that subsequent loss leaves the transplanted island isolated in a sea of scalp, like a photographic negative of a monk's ring. Of course, I don't claim any medical expertise in this area, but I would also imagine that a further side-effect of having your head sliced open would be, to use the condition's correct scientific term, shitting yourself.

The only well-documented cure for baldness not endorsed in the national press by Jimmy White would seem to be the bat technique. This involves the purchase of a peculiar frame on which the sufferer is strapped and suspended with his feet pointing upwards. The resultant rush of blood to the head is then intended to stimulate growth, although I suppose there's always the chance that the hair is in there somewhere and just needs a little help from gravity to coax it out. There are numerous aficionados who will testify to the success of this inverse suspension, and I'm sure it's the failsafe way of solving the problem. No one's going to see your bald spot if you're hanging upside down with your head an inch from the ground. It's going to look a bit odd down the pub, though. I think Jimmy White is just going to have to accept the inevitable: many of us are going bald and, as of this moment, there's not a lot we can do about it. If you're a member of a band and patches of your hair begin to fall out, then turn it to your advantage. Use superglue to attach small mirrors to the areas of bald skin, and when a stage spotlight catches your bonce you will produce an intoxicating mirror-ball effect. Otherwise, just be stoic as you stand on the dockside of demi-wave waving your tresses goodbye.

It's also worth considering Elton John. I don't know what he's got up there, but it makes him look like Captain Mainwaring dressed up as Pam Ayres, and for years before that he experimented with what I believe is known as a weave, which sounds like something that would need regular maintenance from a professional thatcher. Consider also Bruce Forsyth, who appears to have half a coconut on his head. If these people, with all their limitless riches, can't find an effective solution, then what chance have the rest of us got? For this I think we should congratulate them. They've saved us a fortune. Like a painful divorce, if your hair has decided to leave you there's not much you can do about it except hope, in the words of Bruce Willis, that you've 'got a good head shape'. Alas, even this proved a vain hope for a chap I know who went bald only to discover his head was pointed. Bad luck, eh?

The Manchester I'd returned to was on the brink of another musical explosion. The Hacienda had become the hippest club in the country with coach parties travelling from the cultural wasteland of the south of England to sample the throbbing sounds and flashing lights. It was a bit like a day trip to Blackpool illuminations on Ecstasy. Tales began to spread nationwide of the unique atmosphere of the Hac and what a great night you could have there if you managed to avoid being shot. For a while it seemed like the concept of a live band could be superseded as a form of mass entertainment by the faceless DJ, often the best kind, who mixed dance grooves for a rabid audience. Concerts had once more become the prehistoric rituals that punk was supposed to have abolished. Increasingly, people were asking why they should be herded into a concrete cattle shed to wait for two hours until the rock gods deigned to bless the devotees with their presence when the same two hours could have been spent in a collective house-fuelled nirvana. A whole new generation of music lovers was beginning to emerge, and it was a generation hooked not on the élitism of the mega-band but on the democracy of the dance floor. In many ways the house revolution bore uncanny resemblances to punk. Both

161

Mark Radcliffe

had a soundtrack that arrived on the streets and initially made its way into the charts without the major record companies knowing anything about it. Both had a national network of venues which existed outside the regular concert circuit, and crucially both had a committed audience who were there as participants and not merely spectators. Like a football match, the crowd was part of the theatrical event and not a mute witness to it.

As someone who was rooted very much in the world of traditional rock, I began to feel more unfashionable than even I was used to, as it seemed the conventional beat group might be consigned to the past along with space hoppers, drip-dry Bri-nylon shirts and packets of crisps with the salt inside in a twist of blue paper. I needn't have worried. A new breed of bands was on the move, but crucially they were bands brought up not on Chuck Berry and the Rolling Stones but on dance music. A hybrid of house and rock'n'roll had grown in the most natural and organic way, and as it tapped into the consciousness of both the gnarled old rocker and the bright young raver it had to be a winner. Manchester was in the process of becoming 'Madchester', and record company A & R people began to arrive at Piccadilly Station hoping to sign one of the dozens of bands who overnight became adept exponents of the new genre. Lots of acts got deals at that time, and I hope they invested wisely, but there were only two names that mattered: Stone Roses and Happy Mondays.

Happy Mondays were a bunch of Dickensian ne'er-do-wells from Little Hulton. Their Fagin figure was Shaun Ryder, a front man who even now you would hesitate to call a singer. Here again, though, was someone who both symbolised something new while simultaneously reactivating the past.

Every time he opened his mouth to perform, you could guarantee that someone would say, 'That's not singing. He can't hold a tune to save his life,' which is exactly what they'd said about Johnny Rotten just over a decade earlier. The Mondays had the standard bass, drums, guitar and keyboards behind their hook-nosed leader, but crucially, at his side, they had the talismanic Bez. If one of the tenets of punk was being allowed to be up on stage without any discernible musical ability, then it was alive and well in Bez, despite the fact that Bez himself looked anything but alive and well. With his cropped hair, baggy shorts and unamplified maracas, he prowled the stage, fixing the audience with a bug-eyed stare, performing his signature dance, which, with all the grace of a spider who's recently escaped from a beer glass, sent all his limbs in different directions at the same time. Unlike Chas Smash of Madness, Bez made no attempt to sing, he was just a presence, and without him it wouldn't have been the same. Like the bare-breasted Stacia of Hawkwind, he became an icon for just being there, and if you read the credits for the band's *pièce de résistance*, *Pills Thrills 'n' Bellyaches*, it's there in print for all to see:

> *Shaun Ryder — lyrics and vocals*
> *Paul Ryder — bass guitar*
> *Mark Day — lead and rhythm guitar*
> *Paul Davis — keyboards and programs*
> *Gary Whelan — drums*
> *Bez — Bez*

Musically, they seemed to have absorbed every vital influence of the last thirty years from house and punk to funk and folk, and yet there was nothing studied about it. They weren't musos, they were mates on the make. Like all great bands, they were far more than the sum total of their parts and had that knack of making things that shouldn't fit together fit perfectly. Like Bowie's 'Heroes', there was a sense that everybody was playing a different song at a different speed at the same time, and yet somehow creating something effortlessly glorious.

In the early days the Stone Roses were a more conventional rock band with, never a smart move, an undeniable essence of Goth. Musically, they had two aces in their pack. With apologies to the great Bill Nelson, in John Squire they had the man described by journalist John Robb as the world's first non-macho guitar hero, and there's something in that to be sure. John Squire appeared to be able to play anything he wanted, and you can't help thinking that if he'd been in Led Zeppelin he wouldn't have been out of his depth. He'd have had to fight John Paul Jones for 'the quiet one' tag, but musically he'd have more than held his own, although in groups as big as the Zep there would always be someone to hold your own for you if you couldn't be bothered holding it yourself. The Roses' other world-class player was Reni, the drummer. If one man combined rock bluster with dance beats, it was Reni. The first time I saw the Stone Roses they were appearing with a comedian from Oldham called Bob Dillinger, who was, to use showbiz parlance, dying on his arse. Obviously fed up with waiting to get on, Reni walked on stage, plonked himself down behind his kit and started playing on his own. It wasn't the most sensitive way of informing the unfortunate Dillinger that his spot was over, but it was no less impressive for that. Up front, the Roses' formation relied on a lone striker in Ian Brown. For a while this pouting loose-limbed gargoyle with the epoch-defining fringe was what Mods would have referred to as 'the face'. Song titles like 'I Am the Resurrection' and 'I Wanna Be Adored' demonstrated how the Roses had a self-belief that bordered on arrogance, and it was Brown's unruffled swagger that enabled them to carry it off. He couldn't sing, of course, which, as we've seen, hardly makes him unique among front men, but whereas Rotten or Ryder had replaced singing with a distinctive primordial yowl, Brown just sang in a weak, flat drone. Strangely, this seemed to fit perfectly on the early recordings, which sound wonderful to this day, but as time went on and the Squire-marshalled musicians began to assemble a noise of Zeppelinesque proportions, the Brown larynx became wholly inadequate. However, the Roses will for ever have their place in history as an explosive live act and creators not only of a fine début album but also of a true classic in the single 'Fool's Gold'. Like a lot of the Mondays' material, on paper this song just doesn't work. Brown's introverted vocal wends its way through Reni's reworking of James Brown's 'Funky Drummer', accompanied by rumbling dub bass interspersed with Squire's crackling guitar bursts owing more than a nod to Jimi Hendrix. Three decades of influences are distilled into a few minutes, and yet the end result is absolutely of its time and anything but retro. If you don't know anything about British psychedelia of the late sixties, you should listen to Traffic's 1967 single 'Hole in My Shoe' and it will tell you all you need to know. If you don't know anything about punk, you only need to hear the Sex Pistols' 'Anarchy in the UK'. In a similar way, you can read endless articles and books in an attempt to understand the so-called 'baggy scene' of the late eighties, but listen to the Stone Roses' 'Fool's Gold' and you'll understand it perfectly.

Inspired by this burgeoning rock-dance crossover, I set about recruiting a crack team of hungry young baggies to create an enthrallingly contemporaneous collective who could absorb all the necessary influences and blend them into an electrifying synthesis. I didn't really. I phoned up Wammo to discuss forming another band that sounded like Dr Feelgood. In many ways I think this was to our credit. There's nothing sadder than seeing a bunch of old men attempting to be part of the latest wave of youth culture, and if there was one thing that convinced us we were too old to be a baggy band it was the trousers. When Wammo and I had ceremoniously burnt our youth's western-style bell-bottom jeans as a sacrificial offering to the great god Punk, we assumed the much-derided flares were gone for ever, consigned to the past along with chopper bikes, Goblin Teasmades and journeys on the M6 without sitting in standing traffic around Wednesbury. Gradually, though, we became aware of the hundreds of kids trudging through Manchester in twenty-six-inch flares, the like of which we hadn't seen for over ten years. At first we assumed these were just poor people who'd been forced out of financial necessity to buy unfashionable strides from hastily established bargain outlets following a major find by archaeologists excavating an ancient Brutus warehouse. At the back of the trouser legs the material had become ripped and filthy from the constant trailing on the rain-soaked pavements, so that each crumpled character seemed to be trailing fronds of rotting seaweed behind them. It was all so quaint and nostalgic. On every street corner stood packs of urchins in hooded sweatshirts who, from the knee down, resembled an Apache reservation. As these were obviously coolsters at the forefront of fashion, they'd most likely bought their jeans for £15 from a wire basket outside Famous Army & Navy Stores, who would discover some weeks later, as style history repeated itself, that the high-street shops were charging forty quid a pair. Of course, impressive as these tepee trousers were, they weren't quite as spectacular as the customised specimens I remembered from my youth. In those days the only flares you could buy had a circumference of fourteen or, at most, sixteen inches. This necessitated a certain amount of improvisation, for which you needed a second pair of jeans and a patient and understanding mum. From the second well-worn trouser a V-shaped piece of faded denim roughly the size of a windsurfer sail would be meticulously hewn. Splitting the seam of the pair to be worn, the additional panel could then be sewn in to create the required lower-leg A-line skirt contour. If antique denim was in short supply, the additional panels could acceptably be fashioned from psychedelic paisley corduroy, beer-soaked bar towels or, in the case of an old Bolton acquaintance known as Bij, Kellogg's cornflakes packets. In many ways we were pioneering recycling culture, as no one ever threw away an old pair of jeans, they were simply reworked into ever more elaborate trouser constructions in pursuit of the ultimate flare.

For Phil and I in our sedate straight-legs, the clown-pant comeback was as unexpected as it was hilarious, but it made me realise that, be it the platform shoe, the tank top, the hot pant or the flared jean, if you'd worn it the first time around you were too old to wear it the second.

Not that we'd ever worn hot pants. Well, not in public anyway.

During my southern sojourn, Wammo had formed a band called House on Fire with an affable rockabilly called Vic and a monosyllabic computer boffin called Daryl. Daryl spoke so rarely that when he did summon all his orational skills to mount an uncharacteristic ejaculation, you would have to stop what you were doing and work out where the sound was coming from. In all the time I spent with him, I don't think we had a single conversation, although this could of course have had less to do with his economy with speech than his belief that I was a complete divot. Unlikely, I know, but feasible. He wasn't at all threatening or unpleasant. On the contrary, he exuded a relaxed geniality which he communicated entirely without the need to resort to speaking. He may well have been allergic to words. He was the bass player, naturally.

Vic was the lead vocalist and had many things to recommend him in that department. He had an immaculate quiff, a broad and easy smile, his own PA system and a trailer to carry it round in when he wasn't delivering sunbeds. He wasn't a great singer in those days, but he was wildly enthusiastic and that counted for everything.

They also had a drummer who was unceremoniously booted out when I showed up. That might sound harsh, but when you're planning to play prestige venues like the Rosebud in Preston there's no room for sentiment. In the interests of saving his public humiliation, his name will not be mentioned, which is just as well because I've forgotten it. Looking back, he must have been consumed by bitterness. Lord knows how Pete Best felt when the Beatles ran out to the stage at Shea Stadium; who can begin to imagine what, if anything, went through Tony McCarroll's head on the days Oasis played Knebworth, and can any of us begin to understand the mental strain on that bloke the night House on Fire rocked Whittle-le-Woods Labour Club?

We began to rehearse weekly and, at first, weakly in the architect's offices in Preston where Phil had managed to secure gainful and well-paid employment after a triumph of the interviewee's art of deception. The words 'eyes', 'wool' and 'pulling' spring to mind, as do 'bastard' and 'jammy'. He could turn on the charm, could Phil, I'll say that for him. He was also a gifted mimic who had evidently delighted his interrogators with a brilliant impersonation of a sober young gentleman who would make a punctual and diligent employee.

We sat down to select a set list on strictly democratic lines, which meant that Phil and I wrote down all the Dr Feelgood songs we could think of, while Vic, cheeriness incarnate, interjected with the odd 'sounds great' and the occasional 'nice one', and Dave endorsed proceedings in his silence.

We launched ourselves on to the pub circuit around Preston, performing principally in dingy back bars lit by fluorescent strip lights. These were the kind of places where your shoes would have stuck to the carpet, had not the landlord had the foresight to cover the floors in linoleum designed to recreate the patterns made in murky puddles by spillages of motor oil. Half the audience, on a good night twenty people, were predominantly male blues enthusiasts with a genuine love of live music. The other half, predominantly male as far as you could tell, were cantankerous old soaks in nicotine-stained raincoats and battered brown trilby hats whose principal reason for being there was that a pint of mild was a penny cheaper than in the luxuriously appointed, hallucinogenic flock-paper-clad lounge facility on the other side of the bar.

To label them a sector of 'the audience' is perhaps less than accurate in that it implies that they paid any attention to what we were doing. In fact, they would spend the complete duration of our performance hunched over the bar with a bloodshot gaze fixed on the shimmering optics, dreaming of scarcely affordable chasers or hoping for brisk sales from the card of Big D peanuts, each bag sold revealing further cleavage of the pneumatic starlet's photograph beneath. Their lack of discernible movement and leathery skin made you wonder whether they were the result of some abortive genetic cross-breeding programme involving OAPs in council care and iguanas. I suppose it's more likely that they were too slaughtered to stand up without something to lean on, and I can only assume, from the length of time they stood there, that answering a call of nature in their shapeless grey slacks was deemed less of an indignity than attempting to negotiate a passage to the gents' and collapsing in a heap of spittle-spattered gaberdine and rancid rayon in the middle of an empty dance floor. The only energy they expended was in the lifting of successive pints, the saved penny total rising by a factor of five an hour, and the automaton-like insertion of unfiltered cigarettes into mouths where gaps were interrupted with the occasional tooth. As a circuit it was hardly the most rewarding, but with the incurable optimism of rock'n'roll journeymen we knew that something better was just around the corner.

The big break came one Saturday afternoon when Wammo received a breathlessly excited phone call from the irrepressibly excitable and occasionally asthmatic Vic. Obviously, it being his house, Phil answered the phone, so I couldn't hear exactly what Vic was saying, but I could ascertain from his animated tone that it was thrilling news.

'Yibbee yabba yobba yabba yibbee yey.'

'Oh, hi, Vic, what's up?'

'Yobba wobba wibba wobble wee.'

'Really? In Blackpool?'

'Hibba hobba hubba hubba hebba hooo.'

'On the promenade? Big cash prizes?'

'Bibble babble blah blah bobble bubble bee.'

'Right, then. Tuesday night, seven-thirty it is. See you there.' Phil replaced the receiver and turned to me: 'Right, this is it. Vic's got us a gig at this big pub in Blackpool on Tuesday. Six bands are playing and the best gets a load of good gigs, including the chance to play at King George's Hall in Blackburn. Good, eh?'

'Oh, bloody hell, Wammo.'

'What's wrong?'

'It's a frigging talent contest, that's what's wrong. A sad, crappy Battle of the Bands where all the local heavy-metal underachievers compete for the chance to support the Tygers of Pan Tang in a municipal auditorium with all the atmosphere of a planet in the solar system with little or no atmosphere – for example, Pluto – or a day's recording at a seven-track studio in a converted tool-shed in Fleetwood.'

'Well, there's no need to be so negative, it might be just the break we need. Anyway, I want to do it and Vic's well up for it.'

Mark Radcliffe

'What does Daryl say?'
'Bugger all, as well you know.'

Unloading the gear on to the south promenade at Blackpool that Tuesday night, the signs were not promising. It was pouring with rain and bitterly cold with a wind that cut through you like a dead, dead sharp thing. The pub was called the Star and was located near the gates of the celebrated funfair known as the Pleasure Beach, these days nestling in the shadow of the Pepsi Max Big One. Vic was already in discussion with the organiser about the order in which the bands were going to appear. There were five other acts: a lame jazz funk trio called Colourblind, a contemptible sub-Foreigner AOR (arsehole-oriented rock) band called Cold as Ice, an identikit four-piece indie-guitar outfit known as the Fractions, another equally contemptible AOR combo going by the name of Tanglewood and, favourites due to this being a home tie for them, local heavy-metal underachievers the Cannibals. The running order having been settled by the drawing of numbered tickets, we found ourselves appearing fourth and discovered, with no great surprise, that the Cannibals were going on last.

Vic was in a state of high agitation and chattered twenty to the dozen, making it impossible for anyone else to get a word in edgeways, which didn't really matter because he was talking to Daryl. Wammo and I had retired to the snug bar, partially to avoid listening to the opposition and partially because we'd discovered that the beer was a penny a pint cheaper.

Eventually, after Phil and I had saved at least eight pence each, it was time for us to go on. In the interests of saving time in the change-overs, every band was using the same drum-kit, a kit provided for all of us in a spirit of true brotherhood by the bouffant-haired percussionist out of the Cannibals. The fact that this kit was set up centre stage before any of the other bands arrived in the venue didn't strike me as suspicious until much later. At the time my main concern was how to tackle this unfamiliar equipment. As a drummer, I've always been of the Charlie Watts school: anything more than four drums, a hi-hat and three cymbals is for posers. I always loved the fact that Charlie Watts was in the Rolling Stones, for years the biggest band in the world, with access to unlimited cash and equipment and yet he always played his trademark Gretsch maple jazz kit. It's one of the reasons Charlie has become the coolest Stone. The other is that he's aged gracefully with his meticulously barbered white hair and sharply cut Savile Row suits, while the others have persisted with archaic haircuts and the sort of leggings, velvet jerkins and pixie boots you'd more expect to find on assorted Merry Men in an over-fifties amateur dramatic production of *Robin Hood*.

The Cannibals' kit was rumoured to have once belonged to Bill Ward out of Black Sabbath, and I strongly suspect the rumour was true. It certainly sounded bad enough. It wasn't the sound that bothered me, however. What really worried me was the sheer size of the thing. There must have been fifteen drums in this set-up, topped by a veritable forest of stands crowned with at least a dozen cymbals. The stage looked like it had been set for a plate-spinning act. Personally, huge racks of tom-toms have always made me nervous in case an elaborate fill should leave me stranded at the floor tom, many drums away from the hi-hat and snare, with no obvious means of getting back. And yet it takes a man with greater will-power than me not to try hitting everything that's available. This in itself presented a further problem in that, being of limited stature, and in the absence of telescopic drumsticks, there were several pieces of equipment I couldn't physically reach. This meant that key cues and accents failed to receive the requisite percussive reinforcement as a flourishing stick failed to connect with anything save the smoke-laden air. The preposterous pomposity of this kit was completed by the ultimate accessory for the dickhead drummer: a gong, and not the sort of plate-sized device used to summon purple-rinsed dowagers to dinner in discreet seaside boarding-houses, but the full-scale J. Arthur Rank-er. It's often been suggested that the striking of an orchestral gong by the steroid-enriched goon with the glistening loincloth-clad torso is the most macho expression in music. Indeed, some psychologists suggest that the gong is itself a phallic symbol with which the drummer boy invites the females in the audience to consider his sexual organs in the climax to the performance. I'm not convinced myself. I'm a drummer and I have a penis, but I've never felt the urge to hit it with a mallet at the end of 'Johnny B. Goode'.

The size of the drum-kit actually prevented me from having any visual or aural contact with anybody, which is not ideal when the basic intention is to play together. We appeared to be starting and finishing songs at around the same time, which had to mean that the others were doing their best to follow me as I clubbed my way around this Aladdin's cave of drums, finding new things to hit at every turn. In what seemed a peculiarly short time, we reached the end of our set and left the stage with what was quite possibly the only version of 'Route 66' ever to feature the symphonic gong. To ask me why I hit it is like asking mountaineers why they climb Everest. It was just there.

We adjourned to the back bar to the distant sound of Cold as Ice, followed by the all-conquering Cannibals, who thrust their crotches at the audience in cocksure fashion beneath a battery of flashing lights which had noticeably failed to even flicker while anyone else was on.

'Well, that was bloody awful,' said Wammo. 'I was out of tune, Vic sang all the wrong words, Daryl was well distorted and, Sparky, you were on a different planet.'

'Oh, come on, it wasn't all that bad,' offered Vic, 'was it, Mark?'

'Well, it sounded fine from where I was. What do you say, Daryl?'

'. . .'

We settled back to wait for the results, a tense time as no one knew who would be runners-up to the Cannibals, although we strongly suspected it wasn't going to be us. Mein host eventually clambered on to the stage and blew into the lead vocal mike, which had probably once belonged to Burke Shelley out of Budgie, and commenced the all-important announcements.

'Right, here are the results of the Star Hotel North-Western Battle of the Bands heat. In sixth place, and a prize of five pounds—'

Oh God, no, not last, please not last.

'—from Preston . . . House on Fire.'

Cobblers.

To see Vic going up there to shake hands with the pustulous and portly publican would have broken my heart if I'd been remotely sober. Here was a thoroughly decent young chap, starting out in showbiz, coming last in a seaside talent show after an extremely poor performance from his ageing, bladdered and uncommunicative accomplices. I suppose winning five pounds would have been something, had it not cost £10 to enter.

I lost interest in House on Fire after that, but not before a twist of fate gave me an opportunity for revenge. By this time I was a DJ on commercial radio and was invited to join several other D-list local celebrities on the judging panel of a Battle of the Bands final at King George's Hall in Blackburn where the much-fancied Cannibals found themselves finishing in bronze medal position after surprisingly low scoring from the Manchester jury.

In a sense, being a DJ began to present something of a dilemma. As an arbiter of public taste, I was free to slag off the work of others at the same time as climbing on to stages to let punters judge my own feeble efforts. Anyone who heard me laying into Spandau Ballet on Piccadilly Radio, and I can't imagine there were many, would, on the huge assumption that they'd given a toss, have been struck with the feeling that a double standard was being applied: 'Who the bloody heck does he think he is, dissing the Ballet when his own band are a bag of shite?' It was a view with which I had considerable sympathy, and as the radio career was beginning to look a good deal more lucrative than the musical one, I considered quitting bands altogether to save myself from ridicule.

Then I realised that, being a DJ, I was going to be a target for ridicule whatever I did, so I carried on playing a bit longer.

9

Various Artists

I don't know who was responsible for coining the phrase 'revenge is a dish best served cold', but whoever it was they were, to use another well-known phrase, 'talking through their arse'. I daresay it was some posh git who thinks soup is a dish best taken cold as well. If only these trainee *bons viveurs* would face historical fact and acknowledge that gazpacho was born of necessity during a prolonged power cut. As if that wasn't bad enough, these cold broth imbibers will often follow their unheated gruel starter with a warm salad. What's that all about, then? They'll be suggesting iced tea next. The point is that not all of us are in a position to be fussy about the temperature of revenge. For the vast majority of vindictive bastards, revenge is a dish taken any way you can get it, even if it is served in a grime-infested cracked mug at the soup kitchen of retribution.

My wilful act of sabotage on the career of the Cannibals kept me in good spirits for weeks, and if any member of the band is reading this, then rest assured I did you a favour in the long run. You may have thought that winning that talent contest was the big break you'd been waiting for, but you'd

Mark Radcliffe

never have made it to the top, because there was one thing that would always have held you back: you were bloody awful. Admittedly, you were better than us, but then there were primary-school chime-bar orchestras who were better than us that night. Look at it this way, if it hadn't been me who ruined your dreams, then it would have been some unscrupulous agent or manager who would have run off with the money sometime in the future. It's every man for himself and dog eat dog out there, as any self-respecting cannibal should be well aware. (Do vegetarian cannibals live entirely on nuts, do you suppose?)

In a rather grand way we retired from live performance after the indignities heaped upon us that night at the Star. We felt that our musical vision was outpacing the limited imagination of the audience, or, to put it another way, we were fed up of being greeted with disinterest on a good night and a shower of Newcastle Brown bottles on a bad one. Of course, the idea of not having a band at all never crossed our minds. By this time we knew that being in one was never going to provide a passport to untold riches, mass adulation and all the Filipino handmaidens you could eat, but it was just something we'd got used to. I suppose there are people who can't imagine life without vigorous physical exercise, or the fanatical following of a football team, or the careful cultivation of herbaceous borders, and we just couldn't live without being in a band. If you didn't have a band, you had nothing to talk about when you went to the pub, and if you didn't have a gig or recording session in the diary, then what adrenalin-pumping experiences did you have to look forward to? A life without beat groups was as horrifying a prospect as a life without beer, and what a nightmare being teetotal must be. How dreadful to wake up in the morning and think, 'This is as good as I'm going to feel all day.'

We decided to embark on a studio project under the name of the County Fathers. In the absence of sufficient finance to fund anything more than the odd day in a four-track coal-cellar with egg-boxes on the walls, this was a pretty illogical course of action, but at least it avoided carrying drum-kits and Marshall cabinets up the backstairs of pubs where our arrival was greeted with all the enthusiasm afforded a team of thickset navvies undertaking structural alterations. The management may well have apologised for any inconvenience caused to patrons during refurbishment, but there were regulars who felt that management should have been equally contrite during our set.

The County Fathers consisted of Wammo, me and former Cresta Jack 'Mad Axe' Carlton, who'd been spending his time cultivating impressively sturdy offspring, a solid career in radio production and a bald patch of considerable proportions. With only the vaguest idea what we were doing, we went into the studio to record three songs and the unthinkable happened. Somebody actually liked it.

Guy Lovelady was a local advertising executive who'd founded Ugly Man Records with his brother just because they liked the idea of running a record label. We soon changed that. 'It's fantastic, it sounds just like Peter Gabriel,' enthused the amateur record-company mogul. It was probably closer to Walter Gabriel, but as other labels weren't exactly fighting a bidding war over us, we were in no position to question his judgement. Ugly Man were a tiny independent operation, but they had some cachet at that point as they had stumbled across Liverpool's Colin Vearncombe, writing and recording

under the nom de plume Black, who would eventually have
several hits, including the celebrated 'It's a Wonderful Life'.
Having made a few quid on their first signing, the brothers
Lovelady should have undoubtedly closed down the label,
banked the cash and looked back on the whole enterprise
with smug satisfaction. Instead the silly buggers chose the
route of admirable but ultimately misguided philanthropy in
aiding and abetting bunches of no-hopers like us. No matter
what we did, we couldn't shake his belief in us.

'We're not really very fashionable,' said Mad Axe, stating
the obvious from within an extra-large Fair Isle pullover,
evidently bought for him by his wife to make sure that no
one else would fancy him.

'That's OK, the music speaks for itself,' Guy reassured
us.

'We'll need some money for mixing,' said Wammo, which
caused Jack and I to raise an eyebrow to each other as we
knew all too well that the only thing Phil knew how to mix
was quick-set cement.

'I'll sort something out with the boss of the studio in
return for sleeve credits and a percentage,' responded the
unflappable Lovelady.

'We don't play live, you know,' I threw in for good measure, although those who'd viewed our previous incarnations
may well have considered this a positive advantage.

'Don't worry,' said Guy, 'I don't think our strategy hinges
on charisma and sex appeal with this one.'

Cheeky sod. He had a point, though. The photographs for
the record cover involved being doused with buckets of cold
water while stripped to the waist, and the session provided
ample proof that, if our popularity had failed to expand, you

certainly couldn't say the same for our stomachs. We had all entered that stage in life where your inside-leg measurement gets overtaken by the size of your waistband. One minute your waistline is a flicker in the rear-view mirror, the next it roars past you in the outside lane and disappears over the horizon. For years I was thirty waist and thirty leg, and it's pretty depressing when you realise you're not even square any more.

The County Fathers' *Lightheaded* EP was released to a tidal wave of media and public indifference. This despite an in-depth three-minute local radio interview with Jack and I – Phil being unable to make it on account of having to collect his daughter from ballet class. I bet that happens to Bono all the time. The interviewer was one Chris Evans, and you don't have to be the brain of Britain to work out that it was just this sort of live experience that allowed him to hone his skills in preparation for being the multi-media wunderkind he is today. The band may not have amounted to much, but at least we made young Chris Evans a star. There were those cynics who suggested we would not have been on his programme at all, had we not only worked at the same radio station but also controlled its musical output. This is a thorny question and one I have found the most effective way of dealing with is to tell inquisitors who raise it to 'mind their own frigging business' and, furthermore, to 'keep their effing noses out'.

With any record it is notoriously difficult to pinpoint the exact number sold. Estimates of total sales of the County Fathers' *Lightheaded* vary enormously from twenty-two on the one hand, right up to twenty-four on the other. Twenty-three would be a safe bet. The eagle-eyed vinyl junkie may occasionally stumble on one of these discarded gems at a record fair, car-boot sale or refuse-incineration plant open day. The eagle-eyed housebreaker may stumble on one of several thousand in the bottom of Phil's wardrobe.

World domination of the record charts having proved curiously elusive, Phil and I decided to have a cooling-off period where each party was free to pursue solo projects, like fitting a gas central-heating boiler or applying filler to the corroding wheel arches of a Talbot Samba. When you think about it, most legendary partnerships need to split up from time to time to reassess their commitment to each other: Lennon and McCartney, Jagger and Richard, Liam and Noel, George Michael and Andrew Ridgley, Torville and Dean, Ray Allen and Lord Charles, Hale and Pace. Well, all right, Hale and Pace haven't as yet, but there's no harm in hoping. Sometimes these splits can be as unpleasant as the most acrimonious divorce, but you see things a lot more clearly once the dust has settled, which for Wammo took a considerable length of time as the old boiler hadn't been touched for years.

In much the same grand manner in which the County Fathers had been a withdrawal from the stage into the cocoon of the studio, that having failed, I left the sterility of recording to return to the concert platform. This time things were different.

The band was formed for the best of all reasons: we were all mates who'd been asked to play at a Christmas party, and what's more, a Christmas party we were all going to attend anyway. This meant that we could still go to the bash, but could get snot-flying drunk for free and a taxi on the company's account into which you'd be poured in the early hours of the morning. Result.

In addition to myself, there were two linchpins in the line-up, both of whom I was sharing office space with at the time. One was an old folkie called Cheese, who had for several decades been trawling the folk-club circuit in a succession of sensible jumpers sporting the kind of bushy beard you never see outside the folk fraternity unless it's on the face of Brian Blessed. He knew literally hundreds of songs, some of them composed as recently as the late eighteenth century, but was keen to get involved in a bit of kick-botty rock'n'roll.

I think he'd begun to tire of the puritanism he'd encountered in all those years playing venues with names like the Luddite's Retreat or the Clog and Copper Kettle. Folk is a traditional and ever-evolving music that is very much alive, but there are those who would have you believe it has no credibility unless it's at least a hundred years old. It's hard to shake the impression that these deluded souls would really rather be living in the Industrial Revolution in back-to-back housing suffering from rickets. They are the kind of imbeciles who will walk out in disgust if you have the audacity to miss out verse sixteen of 'Sir John a'Gaunt's Lament'. No wonder Sir John was lamenting, he had twenty-four verses to get through. Cheese had evidently had enough of performing at clubs where, despite being 'the turn', he was expected to queue up and dip a pewter tankard in a cask of Dollop's Old Inscrutable Gravedigger's Ale with a dead rat fermenting at the bottom of it: 'What's up with you, lad? It improves the flavour.' He'd had a bellyful of sweating buckets over his Martin acoustic only for some grizzly, bespectacled barmpot in corduroy plus-fours to come over and say, 'Not bad, but I think you'll find that "The Merry Milkmaid of Wessex, she did meet a ewe inseminator, oh" should be performed

183

unaccompanied.' It was impossible to sate their appetite for historical accuracy. You weren't taken seriously at all unless you put your finger in your ear, something even the biggest folk artists have a habit of doing. You'd have thought that once you've got a few quid, you'd pay a roadie to do that.

So Cheese was on board, bringing with him Squigsy, a Cajun fiddler of some repute in the Burton upon Trent area. The other colossus of the band was Wobbly Bob Dickinson. Wobbly Bob was a veteran of the Manchester scene and, apart from knowing a truckload about music, was genuinely the nicest bloke you could ever wish to meet. Signed on loan from the Ragin' Cajuns, he was not only a hugely gifted exponent of the washboard vest but also one hell of a triangle player. What audiences loved was the gusto with which he attacked his chosen instruments. Watching him fling his head about as he laid into that triangle was like watching Pete Townshend trashing a Rickenbacker, only it was a lot cheaper because it's pretty hard to inflict lasting damage on a triangle unless you are a keen spot welder. In the history of rock there have been many on whom has been bestowed the title of guitar hero, but I can't for the life of me think of another triangle hero to compete with Wobbly Bob. Over the next few months we'd play at quite a few parties with the line-up fleshed out with various drinking mates, work colleagues, itinerant tinkers, bog-trotting playboys and blond-haired old pals of the drummer working in the building trade in Preston. No show without Punch. So much for the trial separation.

Musically, we played a selection of Cajun, folk, rockabilly and country tunes. Despite coming from wildly different backgrounds, we shared a love of Hank Williams, Dr John, Ry Cooder, Elvis Presley, Johnny Cash and Van Morrison.

Mostly, though, we were huge fans of Shane MacGowan and the Pogues. It wasn't just that MacGowan had written dozens of songs in the traditional idiom with lyrics that read like poetry and tunes that seemed to have existed for hundreds of years, it was also that it seemed to go down a storm with audiences who were riotously pissed, which, for a party band, is exactly what's required.

Choosing a name for this raggle-taggle gaggle proved difficult. Not because we couldn't think of one. Quite the contrary. We'd been compiling a list of prospective names for just such an opportunity for several months. It had become a familiar game during endless, empty summer afternoons in the halcyon days of working for a large overstaffed corporation untroubled by modern management thinking, the essence of that thinking being that to save money you should undertake wholesale sackings of staff, but should recruit huge numbers of highly paid bureaucrats to do it. Substantial amounts of time had been spent christening fictitious bands in an attempt to constructively fill that irritating gap between lunch and the pub known as the afternoon. There was the stadium rock band fronted by Ken Dodd called By Jovi, or their equally popular folk-tinged brethren Ban Jovi. There was hillbilly music for generation X-ers courtesy of Smashing Bumpkins, or close harmony pop from the golden beaches of the north-west from the Blackpool Pleasure Beach Boys. Crooning formed a ground-breaking crossover with progressive rock in Nat King Crimson, while heavy blues was topped with the pure voice of the chorister for Aled Zeppelin. From a meeting of ornithologists of a glam-rock persuasion came Guillimot the Hoople, closely followed by the suburban folk-rock experience of Carport

185

Convention. Curing insomnia wherever they played their flutes came Jethro Dull, long before we heard the heady mix of beats, guitars and samples from car maintenance videos that was the domain of Big Audio Dolomite. Five ageing vocalists in matching outfits performed insipid dance routines as Dadzone, while from Holland came the throbbing disco sounds of 2 Untalented ('No no, no no no no no no, no no, no no, there's no lyrics'). Finally came the triumvirate of bands who were a good deal more portly than their more successful counterparts. There were the purveyors of pristine pop for plumpish people known as Beer Gut 100, along with slobbish synth duo the Chip Shop Boys. In the end we settled for emulating those gluttonous sixties siblings with the Everly Built Brothers.

The career of the Everly Built Brothers was a brief but by no means ignoble one. The audiences all enjoyed it, from what they could decipher through their alcoholic haze, and those of us on stage enjoyed it as we struggled to remember what we were playing through our alcoholic haze. Eventually, though, I began to get bored with being warmly received, plied with freer beer and subsequently driven home, which makes me wonder if I was in need of psychological help at that time. Having retired from live work with House on Fire to concentrate on recording with the County Fathers to return to the thrill of the gig with the Everly Built Brothers, I now returned to the studio for the ill-fated Deep Blue Day before taking to the pub circuit again with the Hunks of Burning Love. Representing a break with all that had gone before, the Hunks were a rhythm'n'blues band heavily influenced by Dr Feelgood and featuring a lead guitarist known as Wammo. Where the idea came from, I couldn't say.

The Hunks of Burning Love rehearsed and recorded in a BBC studio in the dead of night. In days gone by, management would happily have turned a blind eye to this sort of flagrant misuse of facilities owned, ultimately, by the taxpayer. The nineties, however, saw the corporation adopt a much more businesslike strategy where every studio could charge an hourly rate, much like their commercial counterparts in the real world. Fortunately, the new breed of grey-suited statisticians hired to administer these pretend little companies were just as keen to knock off at six as their Civil Service predecessors, leaving all manner of dodgy rhythm'n'blues bands, tape and CD bootleg producers and illicit liquor distillers to beaver away unhindered through the twilight hours. I confess to feeling not the slightest pang of guilt about this. If senior members of staff in large corporations are going to have their palms crossed with dividends, share issues, BMWs and conferences at Skibo Castle, the rest of us can feel justified in taking what we can get. I stole studio time like others steal biros, notepaper, telephone calls, photocopying and the odd computer. Of course, there may be those licence fee-paying readers who consider it outrageous that their contributions should have gone, not towards maintaining excellence in the coverage of news and current affairs or keeping David Attenborough in safari suits, but towards aiding and abetting the production of the Hunks of Burning Love's *Showbusiness* EP. To those of you falling into that category, I would say two things. The first is that the money spent on Chateaubriand and claret by management and management consultants in an average month would easily fund the recording of the next Madonna album. The second is 'bollocks to you'.

Rehearsals were a relatively straightforward affair thanks

to the presence of a far more accomplished rhythm section than we had any justifiable claim on. To describe Deedee the drummer as affable in the extreme would be perfectly accurate, but would leave you little room on the scale with which to pay effective tribute to the level of affability attained by the bassist Charlie Cargo. Music-media mogul Deedee is now a big cheese at a major satellite TV operation, while Charlie is a respected recording engineer and soundtrack composer, so it would be indiscreet to reveal further clues as to their true identities, although their real names are David and Paul. And Dunne and Cargill, but you'll get no more out of me than that. Accomplished musicians and well-balanced personalities both, they must have had frequent cause to question the company they now found themselves in. I was taking care of the lead vocals and rhythm guitar, and while I could belt out a song with a passable approximation of the Lee Brilleaux growl, my guitar playing was, and I'm probably being charitable to myself here, unpredictable. It wasn't that I didn't know the chords. I did. It was just that I was a bit unclear on what order they were supposed to be played in. This chordal amnesia has been one of the recurring frustrations of my adult life, along with Manchester City Football Club's inability to attain a major trophy (or even mid-table respectability), and the global record-buying community's continuing love affair with Michael Bolton. How can you spend the best part of twenty-five years playing 'Summertime Blues' in E and still go up to the B instead of the A? How is it possible to do this after several thousand attempts? I refuse to believe it's an abnormality somewhere in my brain. I seem to be able to cope with other, similarly repetitive sequences with little difficulty, for example unbuttoning my flies before urinating. So why am I periodically unable to retain these simple chord progressions? I can only assume that in picking up a guitar in the first place I had failed to adhere to the old adage that a drummer is not a musician but someone who follows musicians around. How does the joke go? Q: What's the difference between a drummer and a drum machine? A: With a drum machine you only have to punch the information in once. I'm sure I'll find that very funny when someone explains it to me.

Phil, by way of contrast, was, and is, a guitarist of considerable natural ability. Or, at least, that's what I kept telling Charlie and Deedee in the absence of concrete evidence from the increasingly rotund boy wonder himself. If I'm honest, initial rehearsals did not represent one of the outstanding periods of his playing career on account of his propensity for, to use musician's terminology, turning up smashed out of his brains. This was due in no small part to pressure at work, the principal pressure being how he could get all his business finished by lunch-time so he could spend all afternoon in the pub. At first I just laughed it off, but when he attempted to eat a twelve-inch egg-mayonnaise baguette widthways in preference to the more conventional lengthways, leaving large dollops of filling on his suit that suggested he'd been caught in the crossfire of ejaculating bullocks, I had to have a quiet word: 'You good-for-nothing, waste-of-space dickhead,' I screamed, 'show up bladdered again, you great lard-arsed divot, and we'll take turns to knee you in the knackers.' Well, what are friends for? I'm sure that when he reads this he'll consider that I've recalled these events a little harshly, but you'd have to be honest, Phil, my powers of recollection are a lot more reliable than yours in this instance.

The Hunks of Burning Love lasted about twelve months playing some of the truly seminal live music venues in the north of England. We played the legendary Cheshire Cheese on Rochdale Road, where we encored by accompanying the landlord on 'Spanish Eyes'. We didn't know the chords, but that didn't matter because he didn't know the words. Great night though that was, we had other, even more spectacular triumphs. Many are those who still speak of our performance at Dick Wilson's surprise retirement party at the Jabez Clegg, or the night a rabid audience, including my mum, frugged with an abandon rarely seen in the hall of St Stephen and All Martyrs' C of E primary school. We even played a gig in the bar of Manchester's central police station on Bootle Street, an evening noted not only for transportation of our equipment being undertaken by two solid coppers and a Black Maria, but also for Wammo's imperfect negotiation of a frayed carpet tile, resulting in a spectacular sprawl, pint-pot in hand, over a line of off-duty officers and their elaborately coiffured other halves. I don't wish to be unkind, but you would have to say that these chaps looked like they'd have difficulty finding a brain cell between them. The chances of finding a secure cell in which to throw the bedraggled and bewildered guitarist looked infinitely greater.

The end of the road for the Hunks of Burning Love came at the end of a night at the Roadhouse, an authentically sweaty basement club on Newton Street. Due on stage at nine-thirty to an enthusiastic and sizeable crowd, we eventually returned from a nearby hostelry at around eleven forty-five to shower a much-depleted and distinctly bored audience with a hail of feedback, slurred abuse and a B in 'Summertime Blues' where the A should be.

The morning after, I realised I'd reached a watershed. I'd always thought that I'd like nothing better than to play music and have a few pints in a pub or club with mates just for fun. It was as much a surprise to me as anyone to realise that actually, after working all week, I'd rather just have the beer and the company and forget about the music. I couldn't be bothered badgering belligerent barmen for badly attended, badly paid, badly performed gigs in badly painted, badly lit back bars any more. Nevertheless it seemed almost inconceivable that I was about to give up being in a band with Phil Walmsley. We were soul mates of fifteen years' standing and as a guitarist he'd just got better and better. Like a fine vintage wine in a dusty cellar, he'd improved with age and spent a great deal of time lying motionless and horizontal. Still, I wasn't proposing jacking in our friendship, it was just that I realised my playing days were over.

'You'll miss it,' said Wammo, 'it's in your blood.'

'I'm having a transfusion.'

'You'll be back doing it again before long.'

'I won't, you know.'

As it happened, he was right.

For once.

The gig that fired me up all over again happened about a year later, and it wasn't Lights Out featuring Wammo and Vic at the Bull's Head in Stockport. Not that they were anything less than really rather good, if you overlooked the saxophonist's trousers. No, the figure who came to exert a

191

powerful influence on me was a man who'd first proved a major inspiration over twenty years earlier. Which rules out the singer in Judas Priest.

While pursuing a spectacularly unsuccessful career in rock'n'roll I had, for some time, been cultivating a relatively lucrative sideline as a disc jockey on Radio One. Most aspiring musicians will have a trade to fall back on, and mine was annoying people in between pop records. I was at this point employed four nights a week to present an eclectic mix of live bands, poets, comedians, forgotten psychedelia and sound effects of breaking wind in the peak listening time that all stations acknowledge is between ten o'clock and midnight. Little did I know it at the time, but my three-and-a-half-year tenure of that most coveted slot would prove to be the summit of my success before being unceremoniously shunted into the showbusiness sidings to front a show going out at the ungodly hour of seven in the morning. I mean, come on, who's going to listen at a ridiculous time like that? Milkmen, postmen, insomniacs and long-term residents of psychiatric institutions who've failed to receive sufficient sedation, that's who.

All manner of swots, divots, hicks and junkies passed through that celebrated late-evening residency, contributing to the cocktail of verse, vibes and verbal volley-ball, but the all-important farty noises were down to one bloke. The Boy Lard. So christened because of the then large and wobbly belly he carried around on the front of his body, possibly on behalf of a skinny old man in a benevolent act of beer-gut surrogacy, Lard's real name is Marc Riley. He had come with me shrink-wrapped from the old Radio Five, and was revered as a bona fide cult figure thanks to the part he played in the career of legendary Manchester comedy-show band the Fall. His distinctive approach to a variety of instruments ranging from the six-string treble guitar to the four-string bass can still be heard to this day on such defining Fall moments as 'Hedgehog Gasometer Leg-Iron Syndrome' and 'Trolleybus Tea-kettle Leprechaun Complex'. Perhaps Marc's most lasting and telling contribution to the band, though, came in 1982 when he left, leaving the distraught remaining members, notably Riley acolyte Mark E. 'Smiffy' Smith (himself later immortalised in the Television album *Mark E. Moon*), to struggle on without their guiding light, a struggle that continues to this day with the imminent release of the group's 537th album, *Hip-Archbishop Stick-Insect Spitball Conspiracy Live at the Horse Trials*.

Lard and I became practically inseparable for a while. We began to go everywhere together, which our other friends thought cute when it involved pubs and gigs and slightly alarming when it involved caravan parks and public lavatories. Our partnership was a perfect match of opposites. He was tall, of constant good humour and the life and soul of the open-plan office. I was a small, miserable git who sat in a room on his own. Somehow, though, when we got together the creative sparks really flew, which is pretty much what you expect if both take a night-school course in arc welding.

Not since meeting Phil Walmsley in 1976 had I had a proper best mate, and it not only felt great but made working for a living a hell of a lot more fun.

Back in those heady days of evening broadcasting, we used to ensure the steady flow of creativity by organising regular think-tanks. Initially we thought once every eighteen months would be about right, but such was the programme's voracious appetite for quality items that the think-tank became an annual event. (Incidentally, the think-tank in question is now located in reception and filled with tropical fish swimming aimlessly back and forth over a novelty ceramic bridge, though what use a fish would have for a bridge is a puzzle to me.)

It was at one of these think-tanks that Lard made his cataclysmic suggestion: 'Blimey charlie. Oops-a-daisy maisie. Fancy a brew?' he began, his conversation often made up entirely of catchphrases. 'Dave Bowie out of the Dave Bowie band has got a new album out and apparently it's his best for years.'

This, to be frank, wasn't saying a great deal. After making a series of albums pretty much unmatchable for innovative songwriting throughout the seventies, the eighties had been characterised by patchy affairs like *Never Let Me Down* and *Tonight*, often referred to by musicologists as crap. The new record turned out to be a gloriously overblown futuristic concept album in the timeless *Ziggy Stardust* and *Diamond Dogs* tradition. A nightmare vision of post-millennium plumbing, it was called *Outside Toilet*, although this was shortened to simply *Outside* on release.

'Ooh, my life,' continued the bulbous one. 'Apparently he's doing dates in the old US of A with a new band, so why don't we go over there and interview him? Cod balls, battered fish.'

Our producer at that time, a woman who for the sake of argument we'll call Lis Roberts on account of that being her name, looked at Marc in much the same way that vets look at kittens with broken legs on *Animal Hospital*.

194

'Good idea. Just one drawback that I can see. What makes you think that an international rock megastar and all-round icon is going to consider it crucial to his comeback plans to spend two hours of a hectic schedule in a small padded cell with you two?'

Lard was undeterred. 'Well, if you don't ask you don't get. I'm great, me. GET TO BED!'

It was Marc himself who got the telephone number of Dave's manager. I wasn't there when he made the call, but thanks to painstaking research, principally investigation of ear-witness accounts and amateur footage, we can now recreate that historic conversation:

'Hello. Dave Bowie's office. Dave's manager speaking.'

'All right, mate, it's Lard here.'

'Who?'

'Yeah, nice to talk to you again. Listen, does Dave want to be on our show? We'll come to you if he can't be arsed coming here.'

'Hang on, I'll ask him.'

At this point a hand is placed over the receiver and it is impossible to decipher the words, although an agonised yelp and a lavatory flushing are clearly audible.

'Yes, all right, then.'

'Well, never mind. I had to ask.'

'New York, September 24th.'

'What?'

'He'll do it.'

'Nice one. Oh, by the way, is there any chance of his complete back catalogue on CD and a couple of T-shirts? . . . Hello? . . . Are you there? . . . Bloomin' heck, I must have been cut off.'

195

So it was that Lard, Lis and I presented ourselves for check-in at Manchester airport bound for JFK and the great glittering city beyond, known throughout the world as the Big Orange. When booking the tickets, the travel agent had told us that, because we were media folk, it might be worth asking for an upgrade. The upgrade is a bizarre transaction which basically consists of the airline selling you a seat and then, once it's been paid for, you asking them for a better one. 'What's in it for them?' I hear you ask. I haven't a clue, is the answer. Perhaps they're hoping for glowing praise and gratuitous mentions in the programme, but it all seems very strange to me. You don't go to a restaurant and order a bowl of soup and then, when the waiter brings it to the table, say, 'I'm with the BBC, you know. Is there any chance of an upgrade to the lobster thermidor?' You don't order a bottom-of-the-range VW Polo and on collection announce, 'I'm on the radio, I am, what would you say to an upgrade to a GTI, our kid?'

Well, it had to be a long shot, but it was worth a go.

'When we booked the seats we were told there was a chance of upgrading, ho-ho boom-boom,' said Lard.

The demeanour of the primped and permed personification of corporate cheeriness behind the desk changed abruptly. She wrinkled her nose and narrowed her eyes as if detecting the aroma of German shepherd excrement on a size-eleven Doc Marten, which we subsequently realised was exactly what excess baggage Lard had brought with him to the terminal. The idea of allowing the three of us into the Club Class cabin evidently filled her with horror, and it's quite possible that the colour drained from her cheeks, although it's difficult to be sure with someone wearing that much make-up.

'Well, I'll see what I can do, but you can't possibly be considered for an upgrade dressed like that,' she said with some disdain.

We were dressed as any sensible long-haul passenger is, in clothes designed primarily for comfort. Only the clinically insane or heavy-metal bands from the West Midlands, and occasionally a combination of the two, would board a trans-atlantic plane in skin-tight leathers and cowboy boots. We were wearing entirely unremarkable sweatshirts and jogging pants, although Lard's Dead Kennedys T-shirt may have been ill-advised in retrospect.

'Well, what do you suggest we wear?'

'A collar and tie would help.'

'But our bags have been checked in.'

'Well, there's nothing you can do, then. Come back when the aircraft is fully loaded and I'll let you know.'

Wandering in the direction of the bar, we passed a franchise outlet of a high-street chain I'm not at liberty to name here, but which sells ties admirably displayed on racks. I looked at Lis. Lis looked at me. Lard looked into the middle distance.

'Are you thinking what I'm thinking?' said Lis.

'I think I might be thinking what you're thinking,' I said.

'What?' said Lard.

Rushing into the shop, we breathlessly explained our pre-dicament to the assistant, who was genuinely, and fortunately, the most helpful person I've ever encountered behind a shop counter. Lard and I quickly selected silk blouses and large kipper ties emblazoned with screened images of what looked suspiciously like kippers. We promptly donned our new purchases right there in the shop, giving everyone a glimpse of our gibbering stomachs and causing a sudden mass loss of appetite in the adjacent cafeteria. Kitting Lis out proved more difficult due to the fact that there were no women's clothes in the shop at all.

'Hang on a minute,' said the angel at the till. Rummaging in the cupboards located under the tie racks, she eventually emerged with a plastic carrier bag, from which she produced a brown and orange plaid skirt. 'I keep this here in case of emergencies. You can borrow it if you promise to return it.'

One short visit to the ladies' toilets later (Lis, that is, not myself and Lard), we re-presented ourselves for inspection at check-in. The representative of the fashion police (airborne division) looked us up and down, evidently thinking 'Silk shirt, kipper tie, tracksuit bottoms and moccasins – now that's what I call style', and we were officially upgraded. As the plane took off we found ourselves ensconced in the luxury of Club Class feeling decidedly pleased with ourselves, which couldn't be said for our fellow élite passengers, who'd paid all that extra money to ensure they wouldn't have to sit anywhere near people like us.

We were staying just off Times Square in a chic hotel where the lighting was so fashionably low that you needed a miner's helmet with fully functioning lamp to negotiate your way across the lobby without walking into some disgustingly healthy individual dressed from head to toe in Calvin Klein – which looked very uncomfortable for Calvin. I'd been looking forward to rediscovering New York as I'd been once before when I was eighteen. I wanted to wander Central Park and amble up to the Museum of Modern Art and ride the subway and take the ferry to Staten Island and visit Radio City Music

Hall and pluck up the courage to visit a live peep-show. As it turned out, there wasn't time for any of this on account of having to leave almost immediately for the gig, which was being staged in a suburb of New York located a short hop outside the city and known to the natives as Boston, Massachusetts. Look, don't ask. Let's just say that, with Lard in charge of the itinerary, you learn to take nothing for granted.

The concert took place at a large outdoor arena with a stage in a covered amphitheatre seating perhaps seven or eight thousand, with a further ten thousand bodies ranged on the remaining hillside. Our sense of expectation was immense and even fuelled us through the turgid chuggings of support act Nine Inch Nails. If you've never heard them, you'd be well advised to make every effort to keep it that way, because Nine Inch Nails are a pallid pantomime death-disco act led by Trent Reznor, a prime purveyor of that brand of angst and sense of alienation peculiar to middle-class American college kids. The name alone is enough to raise your suspicions. Trent Reznor. It's not a real name, is it? It's one of these Stateside names like Meryl Streep which you feel sure must be anagrams. The eminent Mr Reznor also employed some dubious shock tactics in his recording locations. One of his collections of platinum-selling dirges was recorded at the house on Cielo Drive where Charles Manson's family had brutally murdered Roman Polanski's pregnant film-starlet wife, Sharon Tate, along with three of her friends and a young bloke who had the misfortune to be visiting his mate in the nearby gatehouse. Trent later denied he had any knowledge of this, and one can only guess at his surprise when he learnt the truth. There you are renting a luxury holiday home to get a bit of peace and quiet and write a few songs, and it turns out to be the scene of one of the most notorious blood-baths of the late twentieth century. Bad luck and no mistake.

Shifting uncomfortably from one buttock to another, we were just beginning to get restless when suddenly, in a black leather suit, there he was. As he walked almost nonchalantly downstage, crooning as he came, the audience reaction was nothing short of rabid, although, of course, you would have to say that the vast majority of Americans will whoop and holler at the opening of a bag of crisps. For myself, I couldn't move or speak at all, let alone whoop and holler. David Bowie had materialised in front of me and I was fourteen years old all over again.

He had a new band, although long-standing guitarist Carlos Alomar was a comforting presence, as was Mike Garson, veteran pianist in the court of King Dave and celebrated for his psychotic solos, most notably on 'Aladdin Sane'. Newer recruits included lead guitar strangler Reeves Gabrels, supplier of textures more than a little redolent of the great Robert Fripp, and bassist Gail Ann Dorsey, with whom Bowie duetted to devastating effect on 'Under Pressure'. He played lots of stuff from the new album and a few old favourites, too, including a radical reworking of 'The Man Who Sold the World'. There was even a bit of daft dicking about with chairs and mannequins. It was wonderful.

We flew back to New York and I decided to go and check out the studio we'd be using to broadcast the programme the next day. As Lis discussed technical requirements with the engineers, and Lard discussed the location of the nearest bar with the janitor, I sat in the control room and began to map out the questions I'd ask the closest thing I'd ever had to a hero. The others eventually went back to the hotel, but I stayed on, filling the gathering gloom with Silk Cut smoke and taking stock of the moment. Here I was, sitting alone in a room just off Broadway, and tomorrow, sitting with me in the same room, would be David Bowie.

The next morning we met at a diner on the corner of Time Square and had a late breakfast of triple pastrami eggs over easy on rye with Swiss accompanied by grandslam griddle pancake'n'grits with blueberry hash-brown muesli muffins. Or something. We didn't speak much. I was nervous and Lard had his mouth full, which left Lis with no one to talk to.

At the studio I checked through all the records and questions and made sure I knew how the equipment worked. The last thing I wanted was for Bowie to think I was a gormless incompetent, although if he'd heard our shows it was obviously going to be too late to worry about that. The three of us sat in the green-room to wait, drinking coffee we didn't want, which only made us more hyperactive than we already were. And then suddenly, like Boston the night before and the Manchester Hardrock in 1973, there he was. He had, I think, a manager and a personal assistant with him, but I can't be sure. I didn't notice anyone else. There was certainly no entourage, no posse of over-attentive pluggers, no massed ranks of surly security guards. David Bowie was in the same room as me for the third time in my life, but this time he wasn't yards away behind a fence of footlights, monitors and crash barriers, he was walking towards me offering his hand. I almost committed the *faux pas* of kissing his ring.

'Hi, Mark, I'm David.'

Bloody hell, mate, I know who you are.

He was smaller in real life, but then many of the biggest rock stars are. I remember seeing Jon Bon Jovi in the flesh and watching with interest as his tour manager smuggled him out of the venue in a shopping-bag. He didn't really, I made that up. It was a suitcase.

Bowie had had long years of well-documented battles against all manner of addictions, in which case he had no right to look as fabulous as he did. His teeth had been fixed up, but apart from that he looked extremely untampered with, just fit, lean, tanned, hirsute and as relaxed, chatty and smiley as the woman who lent Lis the skirt in the tie shop at Manchester airport, which is by no means faint praise.

Listening back to that programme now, I'm struck not only by how relaxed he sounds, but by how at ease I appear to be. Bearing in mind I was broadcasting across the Atlantic from a strange new studio with my childhood idol sitting a handshake away, my lack of nerves surprised even me.

We talked about every aspect of his life and career. He made no preconditions, no attempts to control the agenda. We chatted about the seventies, when he was the biggest star in the world, and about the eighties, when by his own admission he lost his way. He recalled his own look of interest in the making of the two albums he felt represented his creative nadir: *Tonight* (1984) and *Never Let Me Down* (1987). He expounded at length the nightmare vision of contemporary life in the fictitious American town of New Oxford that fuelled the concept behind *Outside*. He revealed the secrets behind his working relationship with Brian Eno, and how the first thing they'd done after arriving at the studio to make the new record was to extensively redecorate. In fact, he'd been in the process of designing wallpaper and admitted that he'd tried the new prints out on his wife, the supermodel Iman, in the bathroom at home in Gstaad.

He expressed his admiration for Scott Walker, Frank Zappa and especially the early Velvet Underground. He'd just completed filming *Basquiat*, in which he played the Velvets' mentor Andy Warhol in the late artist's own clothes and wig. In a moment of delicious ghoulishness, he described how the smell of the deceased icon's aftershave lingered on his musty apparel.

He sent out a message to his son Joe (formerly Zowie Bowie, poor sod), who he'd brought up for long periods as a lone parent. Joe was at college in the States working on a doctorate in philosophy, about which Bowie glowed with paternalistic pride.

I pushed him to nominate the albums he'd made of which he was most fond. It took him a while to decide on *Diamond Dogs* and *Lodger*.

He was unguarded, unpretentious and unphased by the prospect of an impending coach ride to play in Toronto or by the proximity of Lard. It was as pleasant and thrilling a two hours as I've spent in my entire life.

After the show he posed happily for pictures with Lard and I. One of those snaps is on the wall now. Bowie looks amazing, like a brat-pack movie star in a gothic horror flick. Lard and I look like two fat lads who've just met Father Christmas. We even took a photograph of his sandwich.

After he left, I phoned my wife back in England.

'How did it go?'

'Yeah, it was . . . ummm . . . good.'

'Well, you don't sound so sure.'

'No . . . it was, yeah, it was . . . nice . . . dunno . . . listen, give me quarter of an hour. I'll phone you back.'

It was as if all the nerves I'd suppressed had suddenly come flooding out, depriving me of the ability to speak.

We adjourned to a nearby bar where ice hockey flickered silently across a dozen TV screens and down-at-heel drunks sat slumped over the bar top waiting for the rain which sheltering from would provide the excuse for not going home. We had plans to go out and see the town, but we just sat in a booth getting slowly smashed. As I sank down towards the bottom of the glass, two thoughts struck me. One was the realisation that the actual David Bowie had come to a studio to talk to Me. The other was that, even in a cosmopolitan city that never sleeps, Lard and I had the ability to find a bar with no atmosphere whatsoever.

Oh, and I wanted to be in a band again.

10

The Shirehorses

For the next few years Lard and I made a lasting contribution to the golden age of wireless. Night after night we created quality items that we knew would delight and enthral future generations. Such was the pressure on archive storage at this time that the BBC might have strongly considered the possibility of building a new shelf, had not a timely memo from the head of finance indicated that, due to budgetary cuts, all purchases of white melamine from Homebase would have to be put on hold.

A regular feature of our programmes was musical pastiche. We would painstakingly deconstruct hits of the day, and while skilfully retaining the nuances of the melodic and harmonic intervals would satirise the lyrical denouement to comedic effect. To put it another way, we nicked the tune and bastardised the words to include sexual innuendoes, double (and often single) entendres and, inevitably, the trademark farty noises. It wasn't an idea you'd call earth-shattering, but it meant that we could mess about with instruments instead of getting on with anything useful. Of course, we were hardly mapping out uncharted territory. There have been many examples of what is known in the business as the almighty piss-take, the most celebrated being the Rutles, Neil Innes's affectionate hatchet job on the Beatles. A more realistic antecedent of our endeavour, though, would be the Barron Knights. The Knights were a fixture of variety television throughout the sixties and seventies, their career having begun in the beat boom with 'Call Up the Groups', which reached number three in 1964. Incredibly, they were still having hits twenty years later, even though the band members, who weren't exactly pin-up material to start with, had not worn well and the jokes, which weren't exactly funny to start with, had worn even worse. I wouldn't be at all surprised to discover that the name the Barron Knights still appears on posters outside God-forsaken soup-in-the-basket dinner-dance cabaret clubs for people who don't like dancing and don't care what they eat 'as long as there's plenty of it', but I would imagine the line-up is entirely different, the originals having long since retired to sprawling dormer bungalows in Eastbourne, where the glass-topped, brass-framed coffee-tables creak under the weight of the onyx ashtrays.

The Barron Knights certainly gave us food for thought, and the germ of an idea began to grow under the rim of the lavatory bowl of creativity, tucked out of the reach of the toilet duck of management. If the Knights could be in a successful band being not very funny and not very good-looking and not the world's most exciting musicians, then maybe we could do it, too.

The Shirehorses began to take shape, but with one crucial deviation from the Knights' blueprint. Instead of simply mimicking the songs, we'd maintain that our versions were the originals and accuse all the acts we'd lampooned of ripping us off. Hence David Bowie pinched 'Space Oddity' from the days when we were known as Aladdin-ane singing 'Bill Oddity', and Nick Cave and the Bad Seeds only got the idea of duetting with Kylie Minogue after carefully studying our time as Dick Cave and the Bad Cheese featuring Riley Minogue, the act credited with inventing Australian rock despite coming from the Manchester suburb of Levenshulme.

Many other pop names owed a major debt, allegedly. Would the Charlatans' 'North Country Boy' have so captivated the fans if the world had already been familiar with 'West Country Boy' by the Charley Twins? Would Baby Bird's 'You're Gorgeous' have been the same global hit if Baby Bloke's 'You're Gormless' had received the airplay it deserved? 'Alright', Supergrass's defining moment on the joys of being young, seems for ever tainted by Doofergrass's poignant study of ageing, 'Feel Like Shite', while Placebo's glam-racket classic 'Nancy Boy' feels less thrilling after hearing Gazebo's 'Lardy Boy'. The much-vaunted blend of Western rock and Indian spiritualism purveyed by Kula Shaker turned out to be a carbon copy of little-known Northern mystics Peela Tater, Edwyn Collins had a hitherto undisclosed role model in Edwyn Bobbins, Monaco had clocked Moronico, the Ramones had their lives changed by the Ra-Gnomes, and John Squire had left the Stone Roses to form the Seahorses after seeing seminal Stockport combo the Shirehorses. We created a whole new musical history for ourselves dating back to the early sixties, and lied so convincingly to support our claims that there were times when even we forgot what was true, although that could have been the lager. It wasn't the most original or the most hilarious concept in the world, but it was better than the rest of our stuff.

Like most of our half-baked ideas, the Shirehorses seemed destined to play a cameo role on our night-time radio show, but it was at this point that the story took an unexpected turn. We were approached by a record company about making an album, and when I say record company I mean a real, big, proper corporation with office blocks and pluggers and high-powered executives recently rehabilitated from satin bomber jackets and pony-tails into black Armani.

The person primarily responsible for inflicting the Shirehorses on a suspecting public was Joan Speight. A woman of plausible credentials, having worked extensively with Jimmy Nail, she knew a quality act when she heard one, and her sound judgement and musical vision had seen her rise rapidly through the corporate ranks. Joining the company as a junior in parcel dispatch, she rose, after just twelve years in the business, to the lofty heights of charge-hand in parcel dispatch. This might not sound much to you, but as any music business insider will tell you, you can have friends in the very highest of places, but it won't do you any good unless you've got mates in the mailroom. You can be personally signed by the chairman of the company and record a landmark masterpiece, but it won't mean a thing if you've fallen out with the bloke who mans the franking machine, who, instead of mailing your creative outpourings to TV and radio stations, dumps the whole lot in a skip. I know for a fact that Kajagoogoo's career decline could easily have been halted if Limahl had just remembered to drop a nice bottle of sherry off each Christmas with Ernie and the lads in loading bay. A similar thing happened with the Spice

Girls. Sales of their second album, *Spice World*, were initially said to be less brisk than anticipated, despite 'shipping out' in massive quantities. Well, there you are, then. What's the point in having all those records tied up on ships when they should be in the shops? No one ever charted on duty-free sales. As any revolutionary knows, the way to seize power is to control the means of distribution. We had Joan taking care of business and it all paid off when we hit the national album charts at number twenty-two, ahead of Daniel O'Donnell's *Christmas Album*. Tapping directly into the sensibilities of the national psyche, our long – (although, at thirty-three minutes, not overlong) playing platter was called *The Worst Album in the World . . . Ever . . . Ever*. The title represented an ingenious double bluff, as we claimed forcibly in public that it was ironic despite a shared knowledge with the listener that it quite clearly wasn't. The press was unanimous in its praise. *Vox* magazine gave it one out of ten and, in pop terms, you can't get any higher than one. *Q* gave it one star. A star, imagine that, just like you used to get for good work at school. It was, however, the esteemed *Melody Maker* that came closest to fully appreciating the intrinsic cultural contribution being made to life in Britain approaching the millennium. Writing not only with a deep understanding but also a new cartridge pen she got for her birthday, the country's most intelligent rock critic, Jade Gordon, summed it up when she said of the now legendary artefact, 'This is an immeasurably important feat, not only because a number of rediscovered tracks are genuine masterpieces, but because the history of popular music must be rewritten in the light of the revelations contained therein.' Quite. 'But this record isn't just of historical interest,' she continues, gushing forth words with effortless poetic grace, 'it is quite simply a beautiful, intelligent and vibrant collection of songs. Look upon these works, you mighty, and despair' (*Melody Maker*, 8/11/97).

She will never speak a truer word, even if she says that Hale and Pace are not very funny. It's impassioned, informed and ultimately pocket-lining reviews like this that restore your faith in the free music press. With such united acclaim, seduction of the general public was inevitable, and sales around the fifty thousand mark saw us topping the prestigious mid-price album charts for over two months. Overseas, the story was much the same. On its day of release, *The Worst Album* was rumoured to be outselling the aforementioned *Spice World* on the Isle of Man.

With such healthy record sales, the pressure began to grow for us to play live and accordingly we made plans to recruit the finest hand-picked team of crack session musicians money could buy. In the end, though, we couldn't be arsed and settled on two blokes who worked with us. Firstly, there was Chunky. Ostensibly employed as our producer, Chunky was a Leeds United fan of ample girth with a style of goatee beard first popularised during the Spanish Inquisition. He was nothing if not encouraging, urging us to 'rock a fat one' at the start of each historic radio broadcast before retiring behind the glass to smoke Marlboro Lights, break wind and execute feverish throat-slitting signals when the links threatened to go on longer than the records. When not kicking filing cabinets in fits of temper, he was a man of limitless good humour who would often cry with laughter, lending him the look of a big bearded baby. He was recruited as the bass player, despite the fact that he'd never played bass before. He'd played guitar, though, and we figured the longer stretches required to play bass would present no problems for his strong yet nimble fingers on account of the extensive exercise those digits had received during their regular work-outs picking his nose. During rehearsals it became apparent that here was a man born to be on stage. He could strut, thrust, pout and scissor-kick like AC/DC's Angus Young, despite an Aberdeen Angus build that would come to test the structural limitations of all but the sturdiest stages. After each song had been practised several times, we'd eventually reach the end at approximately the same time, at which point I'd enquire, 'Are you happy with that, Chunky?'

His response would always be the same. With a knowing wink, he'd tap his forehead with his index finger and say, 'It's all up here, mate.' Whether he was referring to music committed to memory or hair committed to his head was unclear, although, in truth, there wasn't much of either.

With me on drums and Chunky on board, the rhythm section began to exhibit all the solidity of a firmly set blancmange. Up front, meanwhile, the unique full-frontal approach to the guitar employed by the boy Lard was desperately in need of a second instrument with which to deftly intertwine. In other words, someone needed to play the right notes while he played the wrong ones. This was a job tailor-made for our long-suffering engineer, Chris. Chris could play more or less anything. A veteran of the Chester folk scene, he was equally adept on mandolin, banjo, guitar, bass, hammer dulcimer and hammer drill. He was also a much-admired Morris dancer and could often be seen in clogs garlanded with ribbons and bells moving in a succession of intricate steps and spirited hops, which is no mean feat when you're carrying a tray of fish, chips and mushy peas in the staff canteen. On top of being able to play several different musical instruments, he also owned enough of them to stock a modestly proportioned retail outlet, and thanks to years of training by the BBC in seminars called things like 'Jack Field Normalling' and 'Azimuth Dissemination', run by bespectacled halitosis specialists in shapeless brown cardigans, he knew all about sound as well. As if that wasn't enough, he could fix things, too. Any small running repairs would swiftly be undertaken by Chris with the Swiss Army knife he kept clipped to his money-belt, on the opposite side from where he hung his pewter tankard. In rehearsal he presented something of a contrast to Chunky in that he not only stood still, although if you watched closely there was the faintest suggestion of a minuscule metronomic swaying from side to side, but he also played the notes in the right order. We christened him the Dark Prince.

Nicknames are a very important part of band life and can be bestowed for any number of reasons. John Bonham's tendency to grimace like a chimp on stage with Led Zeppelin earned him the pet name Bonzo, while the Who's John Entwhistle was known as the Ox because he always wore a yoke with which he pulled a little plough. Other famous examples include the big-boned vocalist with Canned Heat, Bob Hite, who was known the world over as the Bear because he often went for a shit in the woods, in contrast to the intoxicating Cat, who moved with a feline grace en route to the litter tray that Prince kept by the back door. Sting, on the other hand, just wanted to hide the fact that he was called Gordon.

The dark Prince was so named because he was the only member of the band with anything like a full head of hair. He had luxuriant dark Byronesque curls about which he was quite fastidious, washing them twice a year whether they needed it or not. The rest of us were envious of the amount of hair he'd retained, but wondered why he chose to dip it in the chip pan before leaving home. I'll never forget the look on his face when, backstage in make-up before our sole television appearance on *The Sunday Show*, the girl who'd been patiently filling the cracks in our faces with Poly Filla looked at Chris and said, 'Is that your hair done, then?'

With Chunky and the Dark Prince in harness, we soon put together a set variously described as meticulously observed, mercurially paced and mercifully brief. All we needed was a small club gig to get us started, which is how we came to play the Glastonbury Festival.

I've never been much of a fan of pop festivals. My great-grandad fought in sludge-filled trenches and shat in hastily dug latrines alongside thousands of unwashed, brainwashed zombies in order to preserve freedom for future generations. It seems to me he'd be ever so slightly disappointed to discover that his descendants' expression of that freedom was to spend several days in sludge-filled trenches shitting in hastily dug latrines alongside thousands of unwashed, brainwashed zombies in order to watch the Levellers. Glastonbury, however, is something different. Even though it is regularly accused of being a corporate event intent primarily on profiteering, it is the only festival that retains any essence of that founding hippy spirituality. If you've never been, and it's my opinion that everyone should go at least once, it's hard to convey just how seductive the atmosphere can be. Set in breathtakingly beautiful Somerset countryside, you enter a suspended reality when you step on to the festival site.

Laid out in the mystical vale of Avalon, it has an unmistakable air of magic which the unmistakable air of dope, frying burgers and raw sewage does little to mask. Standing sentinel-like surveying the scene is the tower of Glastonbury Tor. A small, pale stone structure, it sits on top of a conical hill around which a footpath runs in a lazy concentric coil. Steeped in Arthurian legend, the hill is said to conceal a door to the underworld. Day and night the path is trodden by festival pilgrims hoping to discover the gateway to enlightenment, although they're often in such a state that it would make the discovery of the secret portal unlikely even if its location was indicated with several large, neon arrow-shaped signs bearing the words: 'This way to the underworld.'

Going to Glastonbury is like simultaneously being thrust into the world's biggest rave yet suffused with a harmony and idealism descended from the pioneers of the alternative lifestyle, all captured in a picture of a bustling rural fair by Brueghel. The only things you ever hear in the news about Glastonbury are the drugs, the mud, the toilets and the very occasional flare-up of violence. Considering the liberal supply of all manner of stimulants, and the sheer numbers of people involved, it's remarkable that violent incidents should continue to be as few and far between as usable lavatories. The fact is that the English summer just doesn't seem complete without this epic solstice gathering of the clans. It's not just the music, even though they regularly have the bands you most want to see, with the exception of the Shirehorses. It's not even the circus field, or the theatre tent, or the green fields complete with stone circle and tepee enclosure, or the healing field, or the wandering performance artists, or the monuments of scrap cars, or the availability of food from every nationality, or the provision of all manner of recreational possibilities twenty-four hours a day. It's the people. The great British press are keen to perpetuate the myth that Glastonbury represents a coming together of all the undesirables in our society: the spongers, the anarchists, the dreadlocked Eco-terrorists, the Great Unwashed. What they fail to realise is that for every twig-haired, drug-addled didgeridoo carver called Wurzel you come across, you'll meet ten slightly dishevelled, scrumpy-sozzled trainee quantity surveyors called Colin. For the most part, the Glastonbury Festival attracts not those with a tenuous grasp on reality but those with such a firm grasp on it that they understand the need to leave it behind once in a while.

With a pop festival, your main concern is always going to be the weather. If the sun is shining you can put up with anything. With your closest friends in attendance, a reliable supply of your chosen poison and the rays pouring down on your selected grassy knoll, it may even be possible, and I realise I'm being optimistic here, to sit through Counting Crows without suffering any discernible side-effects. Out of your brains on a really hot day, you might even tolerate Runrig. If, however, the heavens have opened and you find yourself unable to halt the slide from your chosen patch of hillside to the mud-bath at the front of the stage, then even Beck, Supergrass and the Prodigy can seem like a pretty uninspiring prospect.

As we entered the festival grounds that Thursday night in the pristine camper van that we'd borrowed for the occasion, it became clear that even though the previous few days of more or less continuous rain had dampened our spirits somewhat, nothing could have prepared us for the conditions that we encountered. It wasn't actually raining, but darkness had fallen and, despite being the middle of June, it was freezing cold. Technically the festival hadn't even started, but that hadn't stopped the whole site becoming a quagmire. A combination of inaccurate directions and Chunky at the wheel soon necessitated an ambitious twenty-seven-point turn in an attempt to get our vehicle back on to the corrugated steel roadway. We knew it would end in tears and voiced our concerns to the driver:

'You'll never make it, Chunky.'

'You chuffin' idiot, what was that crunching sound?'

'I think we've run over a crusty.'

We hadn't, but we had got one wheel in a ditch. We were stuck. Eventually we had to go and beg a bloke with a Land Rover to pull us out, but not before we'd spent the best part of an hour with our shoulders against the back of the van in an attempt at getting back on our way. Standing there, ankle-deep in slurry with each abortive wheel spin depositing further sprays of mud on to my new navy-blue and maroon anorak (Millets, £35.99), I pondered my first moments as a festival rock star. Lard shook his head.

'Bloody awful, this, isn't it? The festival life.'

'Dead right,' I agreed, 'I don't know how Neil Young puts up with it.'

The following morning we rose early to perform a couple of hours of contractually obligatory nationwide breakfast broadcasting before making final preparations for our much-anticipated appearance on stage. First and foremost we were in urgent need of an extended visit to the lavatory to jettison the considerable quantities of cider and bacon butties that were threatening to turn to compacted clay in our innards. Our camper van was thoroughly well equipped and was, crucially, a good foot off the ground, and, believe you me, in that situation those twelve inches can make all the difference between a relatively comfortable night's sleep and waking up in the company of a lugworm. On board was a chemical toilet, a Tupperware en suite facility of bijou proportions, which you might think would have rendered such visits to the communal water-closets unnecessary. You'd be wrong, though. There's an unbreakable rock'n'roll rule relating to the toilet on the tour bus, and that rule is 'no solids'.

Suitably relieved, and half a stone lighter, we made our way to the windswept backstage compound behind the *NME* stage. Magnanimously, we agreed to play at ten o'clock on Friday morning. Presumably the organisers wanted to make sure the festival got off with a bang, and even though it's not the most coveted slot, it's by no means the worst. Poor old Radiohead had to go on late on Saturday night, after it had gone dark, for goodness' sake. As we waited patiently for our time to come, we began to contemplate the reception that awaited us.

'I hope I don't lose my bottle when I hear the cheering,' said a noticeably nervous Chunky.

'No, you'll be all right,' I reassured him, 'the roar of the crowd will inspire you.'

'Shall I say "Hello, Glastonbury" or just "Hiya"?' said Lard, ever attentive to detail.

'What if no one's turned up?' muttered the Dark Prince.

Christ, that was worth thinking about. When you imagine playing at a festival, you envisage a sea of people stretching almost to the horizon with banners held aloft and the most enthusiastic fans clambering on to each others' shoulders or stage-diving into the seething fray. What would we feel like if we walked out there, arms outspread to receive the adulation, to be confronted with two stewards in luminous jerkins, a juggler in a jester's costume who'd got lost on his way to the circus tent, three bladdered shelf stackers from Bridlington and Colin the trainee quantity surveyor? For the first time we had to accept that it was a possibility. We'd never played live before, and while we'd plugged it on the radio the powers that be had left our name off the posters, probably because they were worried about hordes of Horse fans descending without tickets. We pulled on the zipper-jerkins and matching plant-pot hats we'd bought at cost from Paul Smith, and the new Manchester City shirts we'd blagged for free, and waited.

The weather was worsening. The wind was by now so strong that the hats would only stay on with the aid of a length of gaffer tape wrapped over the head and under the chin. The Seahorses turned up to pose for matey photographs and pick up a few tips on live performance, the stage crew interminably intoned 'one, two' into the microphones, the bass player, visibly agitated, squeezed his scrotum for comfort and, almost without our noticing, they began to arrive. From all corners of the field they came, a trickle at first, developing into a steady stream, which in turn gave way to a torrent. Hundreds, no, thousands of people striding towards a silent stage to see an unbilled, untested, untalented band of misshapen radio hacks. There was even a banner fluttering in the morning mist proclaiming the legend 'Ride On Shirehorses'. When we arrived on stage with maximum pomposity to the strains of Wagner's 'Ride of the Valkyries' twenty minutes later, there must have been five thousand misguided souls with nothing better to do in attendance. I've got a tape of the whole event, and when Lard walks up to the microphone and shouts 'Hiya' the massed response still sends a shiver down my spine and into the crack of my bottom.

By and large we acquitted ourselves fairly honourably, in that none of the songs ground to a halt and nobody, not even Chunky, made a blunderingly obvious mistake, or, in bandspeak, dropped a major bollock. We didn't talk much, to the crowd or to each other. I don't think any of us could quite believe that we were actually there. It was over in just under half an hour, yet so great was the number of people there to witness this historic event that the already soggy underfoot conditions at the front of the arena had deteriorated to such an extent that the stage itself had begun to sink. A hazardous situation exacerbated by the relentlessly pogoing Chunkster. As we took leave of our audience, neither we nor they had any way of knowing that there would be a six-hour hiatus while the authorities made the area safe enough for proceedings to continue. A truckload of shale and a hundred bales of hay had to be deposited into the murky pool that had been created by the stampeding herds of Shirehorse fanatics. The last thing the organisers wanted was for those muddied waters to swallow whole a person of smaller stature, for example Brian Molko out of Placebo, Sean Moore out of the Manic Street Preachers or Ronnie Corbett out of *The Two Ronnies*. With the cheers of the throng still ringing in our ears, we retired to the beer tent, where Echo and the Bunnymen came to pay their respects and our record company treated us to a bottle of Pomagne and a horse brass.

'Bloody brilliant, this, isn't it?' beamed Lard, 'the festival life.'

'Dead right,' I agreed. 'That Neil Young's not so daft after all.'

The villainous music press, riddled with corruption from top to bottom including the bit in the middle, colluded in withholding the facts about Glastonbury from a hoodwinked populace. No one denies that Radiohead displayed a grace and poise all too rare on the festival stage, or that the Prodigy stomped around with an infectious abandon like a bunch of painted gnomes with bolts through their noses who'd just discovered the joys of amphetamines. Nowhere, though, did the scurrilous so-called journalists get their story straight. Anyone who was there will tell you that Glasto 97 was the year of the Horse, or, to put it another way, we came, we saw, we cantered.

Despite the absence of the printed truth, however, word began to spread. Stories began to circulate based on eye-witness accounts of the single most important event in terms of redefining rock'n'roll since Bob Dylan went electric and Half Man Half Biscuit released 'The Trumpton Riots'. Fables of guitars exploring revolutionary new tunings became the stuff of awed whisper the length and breadth of the nation, as did myths of the deconstruction of rhythm with post-modernist dropped beats, legends of one-note bass solos played by a drop-kicking egghead, and tales, quite literally, from topographic oceans. Public demand was growing at a rate which alarmed the authorities, and fearing scenes of civil disobedience last seen on the streets during the poll tax débâcle, a nationwide tour was hastily arranged. The people had spoken. They wanted the four horsemen of the a-clop-alypse to ride into their towns and villages like a latter-day Robin Hood and his Merry Men. In many ways the stout brotherhood of Sherwood proved an uncanny parallel for the Shirehorses. They robbed from the rich to give to the poor, we stole from the rock aristocracy to take the tunes back to the peasants. They dressed in green to blend in with the forest, we dressed in football shirts to move unhindered among the oiks. They lived hard in tree houses, we roughed it in various Moat Houses. They had Friar Tuck, we had Chunky. Of course, we didn't have the same sexual charisma that comes from being romantic renegades in tightly packed tights. Historical rumour suggests that, in addition to his good works, old Robin Hood was a right fanny magnet, with women throwing themselves at him at every turn. No, hang on, I'm getting confused with Robin Cook here, aren't I?

The 'We Came, We Saw, We Cantered' tour left Manchester on Monday, 22 September 1997. Our fleet of vehicles included a people carrier for the band, a sleeper coach for the crew, a van for the gear and a double-decker London bus for the purpose of slowing the whole motorcade down to about thirty-five miles an hour. To give us a fitting send-off, the fine people of Boddington's brewery sent their team of shire horses with dray. If the press had hitherto held back on reporting the wave of Shiremania, then this proved a photo opportunity even the most cynical editor couldn't resist, and reports of that event appeared not only in the *Withington Reporter* but also displaced several inches usually devoted to the angling column in the *Levenshulme Bugle*.

The itinerary had been carefully planned to afford everyone in the UK the chance to see the greatest rock'n'roll band ever. Accordingly the Scottish leg of the tour took place that

night in Newcastle upon Tyne just outside Edinburgh. The
hardy souls of the red and white rose came to pay homage
in Leeds, and those unfortunate enough to be living in the
Midlands had a rare beacon of radiance illuminating their
dismal lives when we hit Birmingham on the Wednesday.
On Thursday we would advance fearlessly into the southern
hillbilly country that lay beyond even Coventry, as our mission
as ambassadors of good rocking and goodwill took us to a
place called London, the capital of Essex. For a final flourish
we would venture into the real deep south, Portsmouth.

Here we expected to encounter uncivilised savages running
amok in the narrow streets, even if the fleet was out. We
were not to be disappointed, thanks to a scrum of inebriated
rednecks from the university rugby club.

As the people's band, it was important to keep ticket
prices low so as not to put the concerts beyond the means
of the poorest members of society like nurses, cleaners and
night-time disc jockeys on local radio. On the safe assumption
that no one would look a Shirehorse in the mouth, or indeed
in any other orifice unless it was absolutely essential, some
gigs were as cheap as it's possible to be, which is to say free.
Other venues charged around the £3 mark, which may not
sound a lot to you, but if you were a single parent with a
fiver to spend on feeding two children and you'd already
spent £2.75 on fish fingers, beans and instant mash, then
it's seventy-five new pence less than you've got, and I
think it's worth remembering that. If you'd had to get
the bus back from the mini-mart, quite possibly a Spar,
then you could be a further sixty or seventy pence down,
depending on how far away from the shops you live. You
could also have found that the economy fish fingers were

222

sold out, necessitating the purchase of slightly more expensive foodstuffs, for example, smoked salmon, Parma ham, pâté de fois gras and sun-dried tomatoes washed down with a choice Pouilly-Fumé, leaving you with a debt of around £35, from which begins a downward spiral of despair. In those circumstances, a ticket to see the Shirehorses might be just the tonic you need, and yet it would plunge you £3 deeper into the red. This would be a perplexing dilemma even without the vulturous touts who were out in force in Leeds charging, for a ticket with a face value of three quid, upwards of £3.25. Poor punters are exploited in this way every day, and how do you decide between seeing the Shirehorses and putting food in your children's mouths? Well, kids are resilient and there's always school dinners to look forward to. The point is, though, that the moral responsibility for the nation should not have fallen on our shoulders. We kept entrance charges low as an act of philanthropy, and those who suggest that pricing policy was driven by a fear that no one would turn up if it cost much more than a pint are barking up the wrong forest. We cared for those people like a shepherd cares for his flock, although without the help of a dog obviously, and if we hadn't been there for them, who knows what might have happened? So much for the welfare state.

The impact of those performances on the wide-eyed innocents lucky enough to gain admission cannot, I think, be underestimated. It wasn't just the music and the stage presence, it was the whole multi-media sensory overload and dramatic innovation that captured the imagination. Either side of the auditorium were giant video screens on to which appeared, not the images of the band a self-aggrandising Aerosmith might favour, but footage of shire horses ploughing rutted furrows. Apart from being as potent a symbol for rock'n'roll rebellion as it's possible to conceive, it communicated that we were earthy men of the soil, free from ego and arrogance, and at one with the audience. We were telling them that, even though we were glamorous showbiz potentates from the great court of cult, we perceived no barrier between us and them, although I doubt if many of them understood, because they were not only pissed but thick as one short plank, which is half as thick as two and therefore twice as stupid.

Adding to the visual spectacle were the two on-stage sheds. A feast for the eye in themselves, the audience watched open-mouthed as, during the first song, the top half of the stable doors flew open to reveal a pair of perfect reproduction horses' arses lovingly fashioned from top-of-the-range plywood. As if this wasn't almost too much to absorb with the limitations of the human eye, the observant would quickly notice that the luxuriant tails, created from jet-black nylon fibre costing nearly six quid, were flicking gaily in time to the music, an achievement apparently beyond the capabilities of the drummer. The tails were operated behind the drum riser via two invisible threads by a chap called Mark. A skilled audio-visual technician and veteran of many major tours, he can have had few prouder moments than this. There were even more aspects to the spectacle. There was the euphoric opening charge of 'Ride of the Valkyries', during which a ceramic cart-horse purchased for £3.50 at a car-boot sale descended majestically from the lighting rig through the swirling dry ice, a sight which became even more impressive when we removed the price tag from the horse's neck. There were bales of hay and horseshoes on the drum-kit and the sheer ambition of the piece revived the concept of rock as theatre. In fact, we can lay claim to having, in many ways, invented that particular idiom. There are those who will raise a quizzical eyebrow and point towards Rick Wakeman's 'King Arthur and the Knights of the Round Table on Ice', but that was just a bloke playing the organ while people skated, which is really not that unusual when you think about it.

The tour was a success whichever way you look at it. All right, I'm prepared to concede that I may have made outlandish claims for what was, in effect, a dodgy covers band performing at five student unions, but everybody got something out of it. The audience had a good night out and we finally got to play at being rock stars for a week, and who would begrudge us that? Make no mistake, we knew we were rubbish, and as for the audience, they knew we knew we were rubbish. What's more, we knew that they knew that we knew we were rubbish. It was a joke shared between us all, band and audience alike, and it was all the more enjoyable for that.

We flew home to Manchester on the Saturday morning with wonderful memories and crippling hangovers, and the Shirehorses story may well have ended there, were it not for the fact that it went on a bit longer.

Enter stage left Damon Albarn.

It was Lard's idea.

'Let's play a stadium gig,' he announced cheerfully one morning, during one of the daily sessions in which we scripted ad libs for our thrillingly off-the-cuff radio show.

'Well, yes, great idea,' I said, 'but who's going to put us on in a stadium, and isn't there just the faintest chance that we might fail to fill a venue with a capacity of sixteen thousand?'

'No, pillock features,' countered the silver-tongued charmer, 'we'll support someone else. Look here, Blur are touring and they're playing Nynex. Damon'll let us play. He's a good lad, is D.'

Well, there was no arguing with that. On the brief and infrequent occasions that we'd met Damon and the rest of Blur, they did appear to be thoroughly decent chaps refreshingly unaffected by their considerable success. Even so, it seemed wildly optimistic to think that their general good nature would so cloud their sense of logic that they would let four paunchy plonkers ply their tawdry cabaret act in front of several thousand avid Blur-ites. Undeterred, Lard contacted the band through their record company and we sat back and waited for the expected rebuttal. It never came.

The office door practically splintered as Lard booted it open with his size-eleven pimp shoe.

'Jesus Christ, you're not going to believe this. Damon said yes.'

'You what?'

'He says we can play Manchester.'

'You're kidding.'

'I'm not, and he says we can play Birmingham and Sheffield as well.'

'Let me get this right. The Shirehorses are going to play the Nynex in Manchester, the NEC in Birmingham and Sheffield Arena?'

'Yup.'

'Well, flip my hat.'

*   *   *

I'd only been to Nynex once, and that was because we'd got free tickets to see Kiss, the grand-daddies of comedy rock. They were on fine form in full make-up, flying on winches above the stage, spitting blood and making ludicrous gestures and announcements. At one point, during the credulity-stretching rhythm guitar solo, Paul Stanley screamed, 'Whoaagh, do you feel all right? I've got my love gun loaded tonight.' Tottering around on platforms that would not have been out of place in the North Sea, stripped to the waist to display chest hair you could plait, he regaled the packed arena to the thrilling aural experience of a straight A chord before imparting the further information that 'all the ladies dig my love gun'.

At this point, wiping the tears from my eyes and with my tongue loosened by several pints of Scrumpy at a nearby spit and sawdust hostelry, I sought to break the Stanley code for any fans who were unclear as to his real meaning. Leaning conspiratorially towards the two gnarled behemoths in Megadeth T-shirts shoehorned into the plastic seats in front of us, I let them into the secret: 'He's talking about his penis, you know.'

From the stage the prophet Paul preached on: 'Yeah, let me hear you say wuuuuuurgh if you wanna see my love gun, Manchestaaaah!'

'There he goes again, lads. He wants to know if you'd like to see his penis.'

Lard joined in, gleefully springing to his feet like an unbeliever converted at a Billy Graham rally, and shouted, 'Paul Stanley has a penis, everybody!'

We left before the gig finished, partially to get back to the pub before last orders and partially to avoid being beaten to

227

a pulp. My memories of that night are otherwise hazy, but one thing was as clear as a long-term scientologist: Nynex was absolutely massive.

On the great day itself, we arrived backstage in true rock star tradition. Initially we'd considered hiring a white limousine, but finding the cost prohibitive settled instead on our mate Patrick's white Ford Fiesta with the rear windows blacked out with bin-liners. Chunky and the rest of the entourage took a minicab from the BBC, yet despite both cars leaving in a convoy to undertake the ten-minute journey across town, we still managed to lose the Prince of Darkness en route. He eventually turned up half an hour later, guitar in hand, having arrived on foot, and entered the stadium through the turnstiles. Here he was, about to play the biggest gig of his life, and he'd had to walk there. Somehow there was something apposite and wonderful in that.

We were shown to our dressing-room, which was in itself bigger than most of the venues any of us had previously played. As we trooped on to the stage for the sound check, the size of the place really overwhelmed us. Often used for ice hockey, the arena floor went back so far you'd swear you could detect the curvature of the earth. On all sides thousands of plastic seats ascended in tiers that seemed almost vertical.

Sickly Rob the soundman's voice crackled through the monitors: 'Right, kick drum, please, Mark.'

I pressed the pedal with my right foot, creating the familiar dull thud, which was followed a second later by a reverberation from the back of the hall like a military salute. It was like playing in the Grand Canyon.

Back in the dressing-room, friends and colleagues dropped by to offer warm encouragement:

'A bunch of chancers like you at Nynex? It's absurd.'

'You're going to die on your arses out there, lads.'

'Have you all got private medical insurance?'

'Christ, that's foul, Chunky, what have you been eating?'

A thoroughly charming Damon and Blur guitarist Graham Coxon, who'd dropped by to say hello and share a can of Kestrel, witnessed the return of our sandwich-board-toting accomplice, Steve. Dressed in a flat-cap and brown dust-coat, he'd been hired to amble among the queuing fans wearing a board that read, 'The end is nigh, but it's not too late to buy *The Worst Album in the World . . . Ever . . . Ever* by the Shirehorses.' You could tell by the looks on their faces that Damon and Graham wished they'd thought of that, too.

We changed into our chosen stage gear: leather trousers blagged from a warehouse in Scotland, near Newcastle, and striped Fair Isle pullovers bought in the sale at Halon Menswear, over the road from the Monsoon curry house. Hastily hired hand Ben the Beard made the final instrument checks and, deciding they were out of tune to the requisite degree, tipped the wink to our ever-grinning tour manager Dave Hardy, who guided us to the side of the stage. I'd be lying if I said the auditorium was full, but there were between six and seven thousand people already in their seats and it looked like the whole world to us. We buoyed each others' confidence with a swift exchange.

'Right, this is it. Let's rock a fat one, everybody.'

'Yeah, rock'n'roll.'

'Hello, Manchester, d'you wanna see my love gun?'

'Christ, Chunky, that really is foul. What have you been eating?'

As 'The Ride of the Valkyries' started to rumble through

the Stonehenge-proportioned speaker stacks, the arena was plunged into darkness and two thousand cross-legged adolescents leaped to their feet and charged towards the stage. The air of excitement ripped through me like an electric charge, although obviously not as powerful a zap as someone strapped in an electric chair or I'd have been dead, which would have been a bit of a bummer; and though I knew deep down it was all an elaborate joke that had gone much too far, it would take a bigger man than me not to believe it was all real for just a couple of minutes.

I strode up to the mike and, in the timeless tradition of vocalists without an intelligent thought in their heads, shouted, 'Yeah.' The audience, to their eternal credit and in a show of collective irony, responded in the equally timeless tradition of the concert-going flock of sheep with an emphatic 'Yeah' of alarming volume. On a roll, I continued, 'We are the Shirehorses,' which we were, 'and we have come to kick some botty tonight,' which we hadn't.

Lard approached his microphone and announced, 'We are the greatest rock'n'roll band in the world.'

'Ever,' screamed the crowd, obligingly on cue. With that, we ploughed into a version of the Osmonds' 'Crazy Horses', with 'shire' ingeniously substituted for the word 'crazy', that was lumpen, leaden, lumbering and therefore not entirely dissimilar to the original.

We played for about half an hour before returning to the dressing-room to drink the remaining lager, divest ourselves of sweat-soaked leather trousers with the aid of tyre levers and congratulate each other on having played to that size of crowd without either collapsing in a gibbering heap of nerves, perspiration and methane, or being bottled off.

Over the next couple of days we played the NEC and Sheffield Arena as planned, but even though we were operating on a scale beyond our wildest dreams, Lard and I reached a momentous decision. We were going to break up the band. For one thing, Chunky was leaving to move back down to London, and in his absence someone else would have to be the butt of all the jokes, and none of us wanted that. We'd miss him, too. Without Chunky it would never have felt quite right. For another thing, we'd played the Glastonbury Festival, done our own tour, played an album launch party at the legendary 100 Club on Oxford Street and performed at three of the biggest arenas in England. What could ever come close to that again? The last thing we wanted was to be playing Loughborough University on a rain-lashed Monday to thirty-two acne-riddled undergraduates at a social for the Philatelic Society. We didn't want to become a bunch of sad old tossers hauling a tired old cabaret act round the circuit, although many would say this was akin to locking the stable door after the shire horse had bolted. Basically, we'd had a great time living out all our fantasies and wanted to bail out before reality kicked in.

I've got the final gig at Sheffield Arena on video, and I'm not ashamed to say I watch it regularly. I love the bit where Lard tells the crowd that we're splitting up, but informs them that the Samaritans are on hand to help deal with any trauma. I love the bit where Chunky is berated for hitting a bum note in front of ten thousand people. I love the bit where 'West Country Boy' grinds to a painful halt during the intro. I love the bit where Lard straps on a sitar and produces the most unpleasant sound ever to come from a musical instrument, not counting the bagpipes. I love the bit where Patrick, on stage with an unplayed saxophone for no apparent reason, lends his fur coat to Lard, revealing a pair of faded, frayed and unnecessarily skimpy black underpants.

Most of all, though, I love the bit where the camera spins round and sweeps over the audience. When you talk about ten thousand people it's hard to visualise exactly what that means, but as the camera pans round that stadium in the half-light reflected from the stage, there appears to be an endless ocean of bodies with arms aloft and hands clapping. And they're clapping for us. It was a moment for which I'd served a twenty-five-year apprenticeship, and every time I see it I relive it in the pit of my stomach. Through all the days of the Berlin Airlift, Billy Moon, Zoot Suit and the Zeroids, She Cracked, the Brilliantines, Bob Sleigh and the Crestas, House on Fire, the County Fathers, the Everly Built Brothers, Deep Blue Day and the Hunks of Burning Love I'd dreamed of it being just like that without ever truly believing it would happen. But it had. Under false pretences in many ways, but at least I'd always know what it felt like to face a crowd's approval on that scale. As far as being in a band went, I knew that nothing would ever feel as special as that again and, with a sense of sadness but also safe in the knowledge that it was the right thing to do, that night in Sheffield I threw away my drumsticks and packed in playing for good.

Then we formed the Mahones.

We're playing at the George and Dragon on St Patrick's night.

The addiction evidently incurable, the addict prepares himself another fix.